Starting Points for Language Arts

by Lillian Lieberman
illustrated by Marilynn Barr

Publisher: Roberta Suid
Copy Editor: Carol Whiteley
Design and Production: MGB Press
Cover Design: David Hale

Other Monday Morning publications by the author:
FolderGames for Phonics Plus,
FolderGames for Math Plus, KinderFolders for Reading Readiness,
KinderFolders for Math Readiness

Online address: MMBooks@aol.com
Web address: www.mondaymorningbooks.com

For a complete catalog, write to the address above.

ISBN#1-57612-069-4
Printed in the United States of America
9 8 7 6 5 4 3 2

CONTENTS

WRITING SKILLS

INTRODUCTION

Starting Points for Language Arts is a book of worksheets and activities for children in Grades 1-3. The book is designed to act as a starting point for learning the basic skills involved in the essentials of language arts: spelling, vocabulary, and writing. The skills are closely tied to reading skills.

In *Starting Points for Language Arts*, the activities focus on strengthening sound-symbol association, spelling, vocabulary, and written expression. The basic tools necessary for beginning proficiency are targeted. Word patterns are explored with short vowel rhyming families, consonant digraphs, and, later, more advanced vowel patterns. The structure of words is introduced with compound words, syllables and syllable division, root words, prefixes, and suffixes. Vocabulary concepts such as synonyms and antonyms and multiple word meanings are also covered, as well as basic dictionary skills. Writing skills are developed starting with simple sentence structure and mechanics and then paragraph development and report writing. The activities in the book enable the primary-grade child to express his/her ideas using the tools of the trade, and to do so with knowledge, comfort, and pleasure.

The worksheets and activities in the book are structured with lesson prompts, keys, and directions. Concepts are highlighted for easy student and teacher reference. The strong phonics emphasis is supported by explanations that should be supplemented and expanded on by the teacher.

Throughout the pages, the children will be motivated and entertained by a group of frolicking, frisky seals that entice them to learn. The seals' humorous capers not only add page appeal but also add to the content of the tasks involved. Also sprinkled throughout the book are hands-on activities and games that enliven the learning atmosphere as well as provide meaningful practice.

How to Use This Book

Starting Points for Language Arts is flexible. You can use individual worksheets and activities to supplement or reinforce your spelling, vocabulary, and writing programs. Or you may use the pages as starting points in your own language arts program. As you use the activities and worksheets, be sure to take the time to go over them with the children, teaching and reteaching to make sure that they understand the directions, concepts, and skills involved.

Most of the worksheets and activities are self-contained, with explanations or directions on the page. The skills being reinforced gradually build, and some of the writing activities follow a continuum of skills that should be further explored. A concept or skill may be carried forward with related pages and activities. You will most likely want to provide supplementary work to capitalize on the starting points.

To encourage the children to become more independent in developing concepts and skills, the helpful seals on the pages provide cues. Illustrations often reinforce learning and can be used as a basis for discussion or clarification. In some of the games, children become coaches for each other, making learning fun as well as reinforcing. In all activities, however, the children should feel free to ask for teacher assistance whenever necessary.

The worksheets and activities are well suited to mainstream classrooms, special education children, and learning centers.

How to Make the Activities

Worksheets: Duplicate each worksheet for the child to work on independently or with guidance. If the worksheet involves activity such as cutting and placing, provide a small zip-lock bag or envelope in which to store the cut-out parts. The activity can then be reused at school or at home. For one-time use, have the child paste the parts to the page.

Games: Follow the directions on the game pages. Glue the pages to oak tag. Color if desired and laminate for durability. In some cases, a laminated surface is required, for example, when children are asked to write words with white board markers. Read the directions ahead of time to determine if additional materials such as markers, paper clips, or tissue are needed. Store all loose game parts in a clasp manila envelope or a zip-lock bag. Glue the playing directions to the front of the envelope or bag.

For File Folder Games, use sturdy plain or colored file folders. Trim the pages to fit in the center of the file folder and glue them on. Laminate for durability. Glue the game parts to oak tag and cut them out. Store all the loose game parts in a clasp manila envelope glued to the back of the folder. Cut out and glue the game title to the file folder tab. Trim and glue the playing directions to the front of the folder.

Clothespin Matches: Follow the directions on the activity set-up. Color if desired. Laminate the activity for durability. Cut out and glue the letters and numbers carefully to the clothespin heads so that they are in the correct position to be used. Provide any necessary materials. Store the activity in a sturdy clasp manila envelope. Glue the playing directions to the front of the envelope.

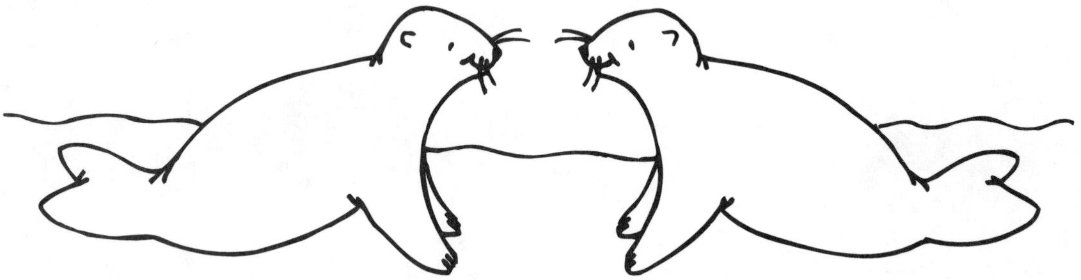

A Nap in the Sun

1.

Rhyming Families: **ap, an, ab, ad, at, ag, al**

Write the correct short vowel word for each sentence.

I had a ________________ in the sun.

cap   nap   tap

Ben ________________ into the den.

ran   fan   tan

I got a ________________ for Mom.

tab   nab   cab

The ________________ sat in the jet.

sad   lad   bad

Matt ________________ in the hot tub.

sat   cat   rat

I like to play ________________ .

tag   rag   bag

Sam is my ________________ .

Hal   pal   Sal

Dip into the Sea

2.

Rhyming Families: **ip, ib, it, id, ig, im, in**

Write the correct short vowel word for each sentence.

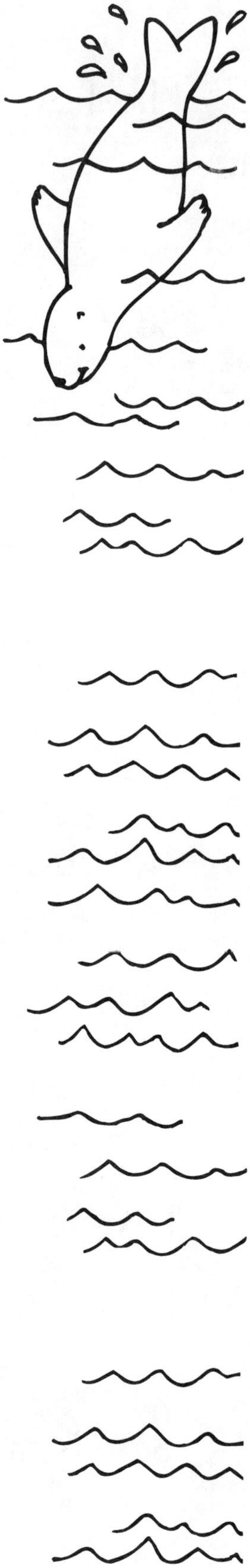

It is fun to ________________ into the sea.

nip dip sip

The dog bit into the ________________ .

rib nib fib

Dad got his ________________ to fix the TV.

sit kit lit

Did you get ________________ of the ants?

did kid rid

The big ________________ sat in the mud.

dig fig pig

Let ________________ pet the little dog.

him dim rim

I put sand in the ________________ can.

win pin tin

Cut the Cake

3.

Rhyming Families: **ut, up, ub, ud, un, ug, us**

Write the correct short vowel word for each section.

Let's ______________ the birthday cake.

rut   cut   hut

The ______________ ran up to his mother.

cup   sup   pup

The ______________ had a nap in the den.

rub   tub   cub

Is this ______________ on the rug?

mud   cud   bud

I like to have ______________ with my pals.

sun   fun   bun

I will give Dad a big ______________.

bug   rug   hug

Jim ran for the ______________.

Gus   bus   fuss

Bob for Apples

4.

Rhyming Families: **ob, op, on, od, og, ot, ox**

Write the correct short vowel word for each sentence.

Let's ________________ for apples!

rob bob sob

Bob can spin the ________________ fast.

pop top mop

Tim ________________ the spelling bee.

son ton won

We put new ________________ in our yard.

rod sod cod

The frog jumped from the ________________.

fog log jog

I sleep on my ________________ at camp.

tot hot cot

The rat ran into the ________________.

fox box ox

Eggs in the Nest

5.

Rhyming Families: **en, ed, et, eg**

Write the correct short vowel word for each sentence.

The ________________ had eggs in her nest.

ten men hen

The dog hid under the ________________ .

red bed fed

The table was ________________ for four.

set met vet

The vet will fix the cat's ________________ .

leg keg peg

The pig likes to sit in his ________________ .

den pen Ben

A ________________ can go fast in the sky.

wet pet jet

The cat's tag is ________________ .

Ted red wed

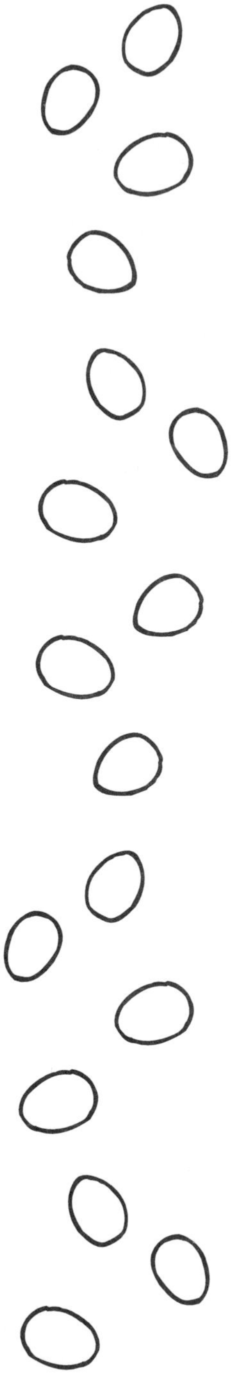

Into the Mud

6.

Short Vowel Review: **a, e, i, o, u**

Write the correct short vowel in the blank in each word.

I fell in the m ______ d.

a u

The big p ______ t is hot.

i o

We all m ______ t at the club.

e a

The little b ______ g bit me.

e u

Dan s ______ t in the blue van.

i a

I can h ______ t the ball with my bat.

i o

My p ______ t is a little red hen.

o e

Spelling Grab Bag

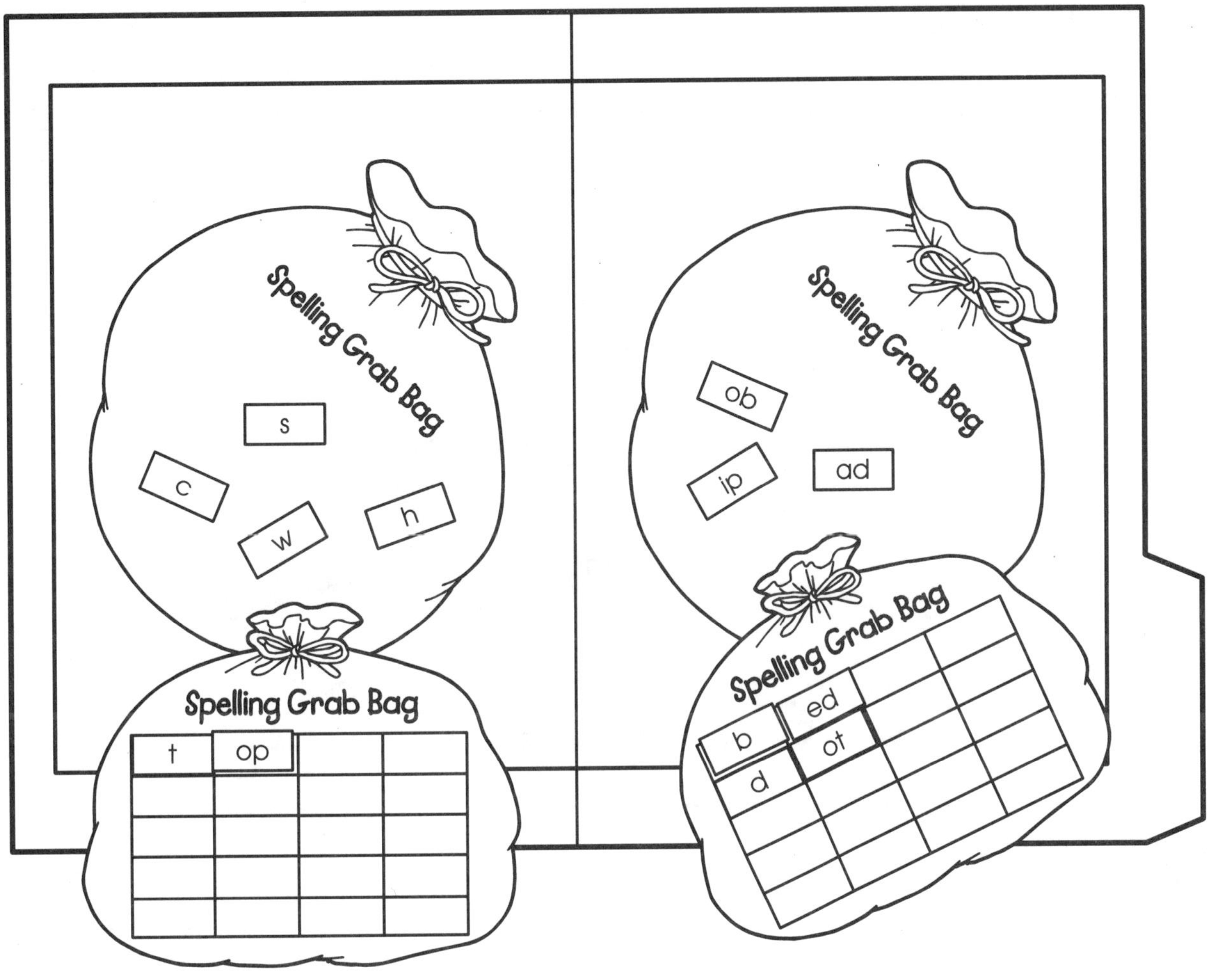

Spelling Grab Bag

Consonants and Short Vowel Rhyme Endings

To Play:

Two players may play. Put the red cards face down on a large Spelling Grab Bag. Put the blue cards face down on the other one. Each player takes a Spelling Grab Bag Card. In turn, each player picks one red and one blue letter card and checks to see if they spell a real word, for example, red. If so, the player puts the cards on his/her playing card in spelling order, then reads and spells the word out loud. If not, the player puts the letters back on the Grab Bags. The winner is the first to spell four real words. The game may be played three times for a Super Winner.

Spelling Grab Bag

To Make:
Make two copies of the large Spelling Grab Bag. Cut and glue to inside of file folder. Make two copies of the Spelling Grab Bag Playing Card. Glue to oak tag and cut out. Glue consonant letter cards to blue construction paper. Cut apart. Glue rhyming ending cards to red construction paper. Cut apart. Keep red and blue cards in separate zip-lock bags. Enclose game cards and letter cards in a clasp manila envelope and glue to the back of the file folder. Glue playing directions to the front of the file folder.

(Make two copies. Cut. Glue to center of file folder.)

Spelling Grab Bag

(Make two copies. Glue to oak tag. Cut out.)

Spelling Grab Bag

ap	an	ab	ad	at	ag	al
ip	ib	it	id	ig	im	in
ob	op	on	od	og	ox	ot
ut	ub	up	ud	un	ug	us
em	ed	et	eg	en	et	eb

(Glue to red construction paper and cut apart. Place in zip-lock bag.)

b	d	c	f	h	j	k
l	m	n	p	r	s	t
v	w	b	d	c	f	h
j	k	l	m	n	p	r
s	t	v	w	b	d	c

(Glue to blue construction paper and cut apart. Place in zip-lock bag.)

Three Cheers for Consonant Teams! 8.

Consonant Teams: **sh, ch, wh**

Two consonants can work together to say one sound in **sh**, **ch**, and **wh.** The **sh** sounds like **/sh/** in **sh**ip. The **ch** sounds like /**ch**/ in ch**air.** The **wh** sounds like /wh/ in **wh**eel. Read the **sh, ch,** and **wh** words.

shop	**ch**ip	**wh**en
shut	**ch**at	**wh**isk
da**sh**	lun**ch**	**wh**ite

Write the **sh, ch,** and **wh** words in the sentences.

The dish has a big ______ in it.

Will you have ______ with me tomorrow?

_______ can you play with me?

My cat is black with four _____ paws.

Please _______ the door.

Mom will _______ the egg for the cake.

I like to _______ with my pals on the phone.

We made a _______for the bus.

Would you like to go to the _______ with me?

Twin Brothers

Consonant Teams: **The Two Sounds of Th**

Th has two sounds—a quiet one and a loud one. The quiet one says **th** as in **th**umb. The loud one says **th** as in **this.** Read the **th** words .

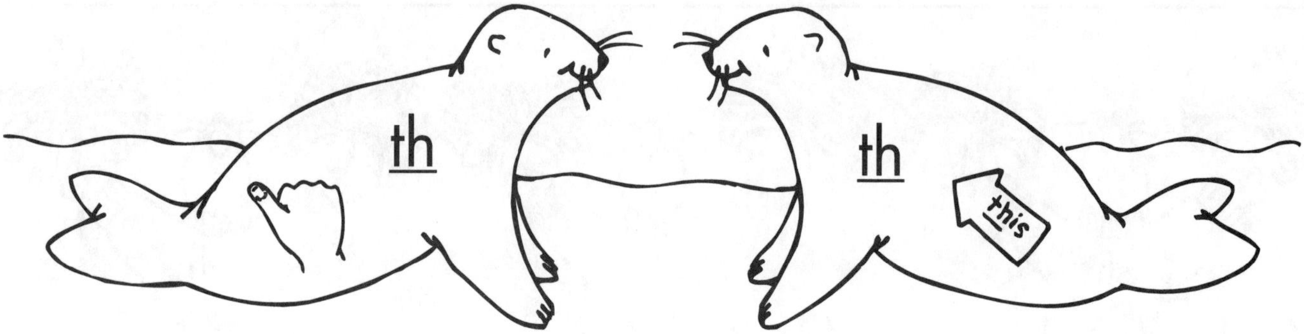

thin	**th**e
ma**th**	**th**at
ba**th**	**th**an
thump	**th**ese

Write the **th** words in the sentence.

Are ______________ your books?

I heard a ______________ in the next room.

I am taller ______________ my sister.

My cat is very ______________.

Will you help me with this ______________ homework?

______________ was a good story!

I like to take a ______________ at night.

Let's take ___________ dog for a walk in the park.

Sing Along

Consonant Teams: **ng, nk**

The letters **ng** and **nk** combine with vowels to make letter combinations. The **ng** sounds like the end of **sing.** The **nk** sounds like the end of **rink.** Read the **-ng** and **-nk** words.

ri**ng**	si**nk**
ba**ng**	ba**nk**
hu**ng**	ju**nk**
so**ng**	ho**nk**

Write the **-ng** and **-nk** words in the sentences.

Geese like to ______________ loudly.

What ____________ can you sing for me?

I put my money in the ________________.

Dad _____________ the swing on the tree for me.

Please put the dishes in the _____________.

I have to get rid of all the ____________ in my room.

Did I hear the phone ____________?

Do not ______________ the door as you go out.

Silent Partners

11.

Consonant Teams: **kn-, wr-, -mb**

Two consonants come together in **kn**, **wr,** and **mb.**
The **k is silent in kn.** The **w** is silent in **wr.** The **b** is silent in **mb.**
The **silent** letter is crossed out. Read the words.

knot	**wr**ist	cru**mb**
know	**wr**ing	li**mb**
knee	**wr**ong	nu**mb**

Write the **kn-**, **wr-,** and **-mb** words in the sentences.

There is a ____________ in my string.

My fingers are ______________ from the cold.

Is this a ________________ number?

I hurt my ______________ playing tennis.

Do you _______________ what time it is?

There is not a ____________ left on my plate.

Please ______________ out the rag and bring it to me.

The squirrel jumped from the _________ to the fence.

Come and sit on my ________________.

Cherry Drop

Consonant Teams: **ch, sh, th, wh, ng, nk, mb, kn, wr**

To Play:

Two can play. Each player takes a Cherry Drop game board, a set of numbered cherries, a word list, a white board marker, and tissue. Players place the cherries, number side up, in the center of their game board. The first player takes a cherry and reads the number on it. The second player reads the word from his/her list for that number. The first player spells and writes the word on the first space next to Start. If correct, the player may drop the cherry on the bucket. If not, the player must wipe off the word with the tissue and discard the cherry. The second player takes his/her turn. The player who fills all his/her spaces on the game board with correctly spelled words is the winner. Players check each other's spelling. Wipe off the game board to start another game. Players may trade word lists.

To Make:

Duplicate the game board and cherries two times. Duplicate the word lists once. Glue all to oak tag. Color if desired. Cut out the game board and laminate for a writing surface. Cut out the cherries. Place each set of cherries (1–15) in two small zip-lock bags. Cut out the word lists. Slip one list into each zip-lock bag. Provide two narrow-tip white board markers and two tissues. Enclose all in a clasp envelope. Glue the playing directions to the front of the envelope.

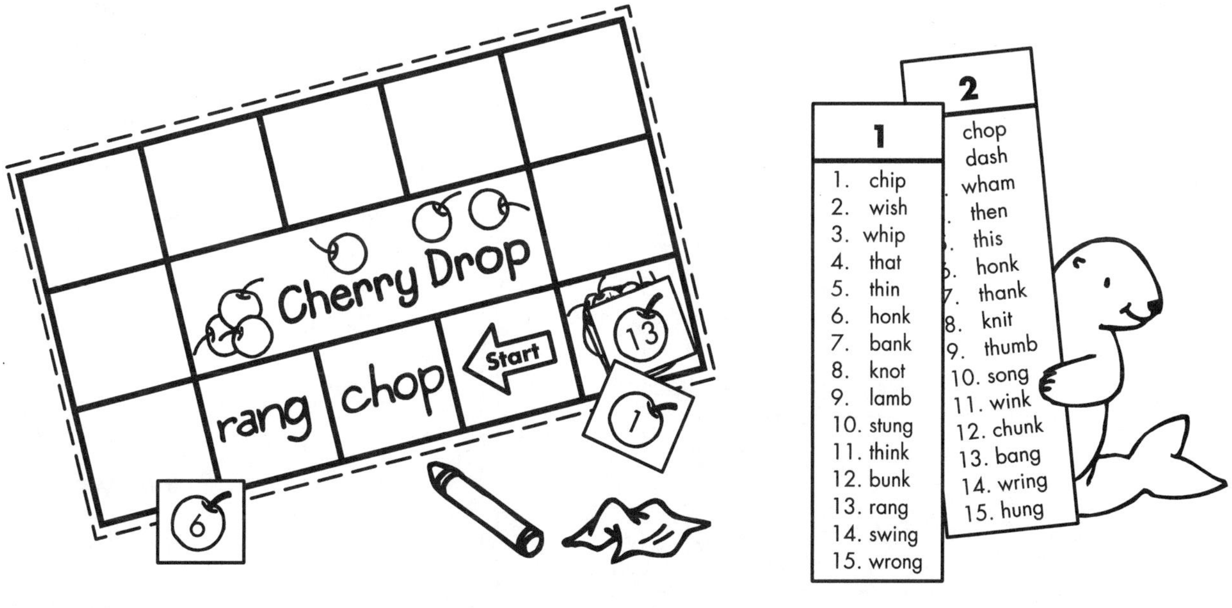

Cherry Drop

(Make two copies of the game board. Laminate.)

(Make two copies of the cherries.)

1	2
1. chip	1. chop
2. wish	2. dash
3. whip	3. wham
4. that	4. then
5. thin	5. this
6. honk	6. honk
7. bank	7. thank
8. knot	8. knit
9. lamb	9. thumb
10. stung	10. song
11. think	11. wink
12. bunk	12. chunk
13. rang	13. bang
14. swing	14. wring
15. wrong	15. hung

First Prize

Vowel-Consonant-e: **a-e, i-e**

The **final e** is silent in a **vowel-consonant-e** word. The first vowel is long. Read the **a-e** and **i-e** words.

c**a**k**e**	d**i**m**e**
s**a**m**e**	h**i**d**e**
m**a**d**e**	p**i**n**e**
t**a**p**e**	pr**i**z**e**

Write the **a-e** and **i-e** words in the sentences.

I won first ______________ for my picture!

Everyone ______________ a mask for Halloween.

My baby sister likes to play ______________ and seek.

The squirrel scampered up the ______________ tree.

My friend Ann and I are in the ______________ class.

I lost my ______________ at school today.

Will you please make a ______________ of my report?

What is your favorite ______________?

Send a Code

Vowel-Consonant-e: **u-e, o-e**

The **final e** is silent in a **vowel-consonant-e** word. The first vowel is long. Read the **u-e** and **o-e** words.

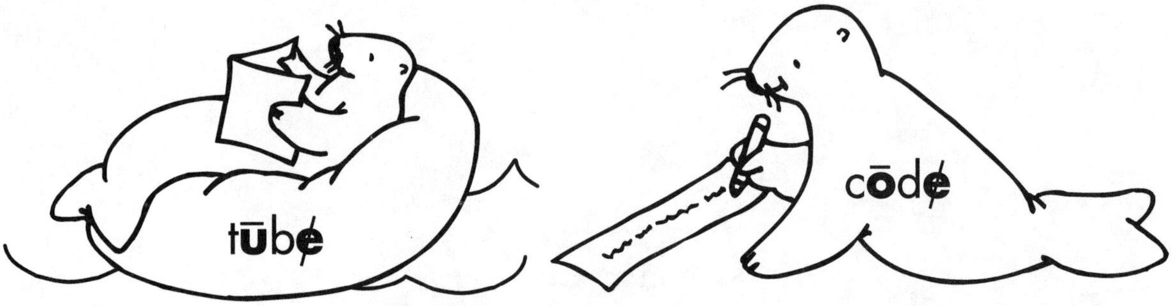

cute	stove
cube	hope
tune	rode
tube	code

Write the **u-e** and **o-e** words in the sentences.

Jan ____________ her pony in the May parade.

I ______________ you can come to my party.

Tom likes to float on the ______________ in the pool.

Our club made a secret ______________ today.

Your kitten is very __________________.

I can't stop humming this crazy ______________.

Be careful of the hot _________________.

May I have an ice ________________ in my drink?

Water Polo Spello

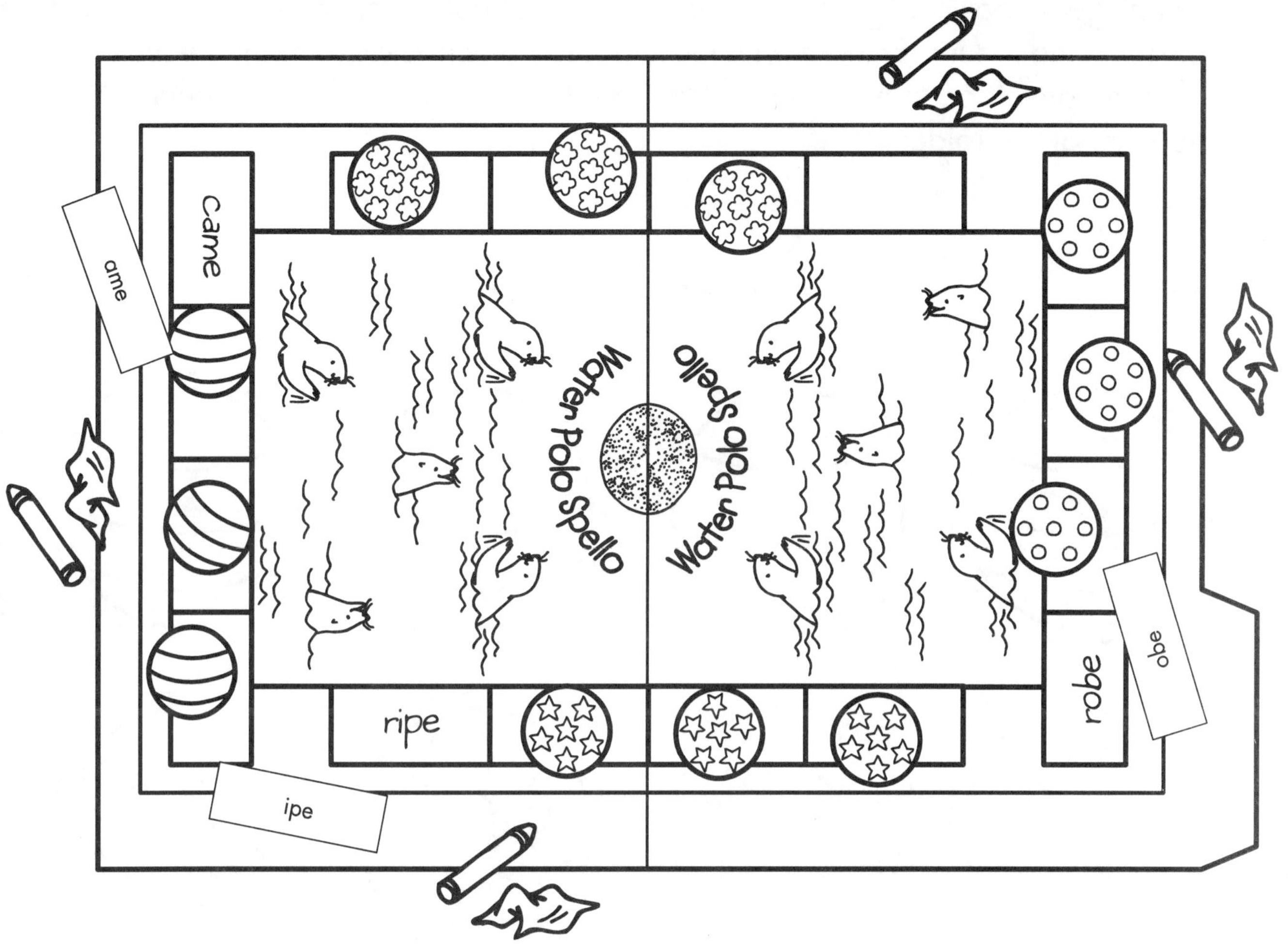

Water Polo Spello

Vowel-Consonant-e Words Game

To Play:

Four players can play. Open the file folder and put the Vowel-Consonant-e Cards face down in a pile in the center of the board. Players take a white board marker and tissue. They choose a side of the board to play on and a set of balls. Players put balls on their spaces. Each takes a turn picking a card, then spells a word using the vowel-consonant-e pattern. If the spelling is correct, the player tosses a ball into the pool and writes the word on that space. If the word is spelled incorrectly, the player loses a turn. A card may be traded from the pile but the player loses a turn. The winner is the first player who spells four words correctly.

Water Polo Spello

To Make:

Duplicate the game board page twice. Trim and glue the game board inside a file folder. Color and laminate. Glue the Vowel-Consonant-e Pattern Cards and ball page to oak tag. Color and laminate. Cut out. Supply four white board markers and tissues. Enclose with loose game parts in a clasp manila envelope. Glue the envelope to the back of the file folder. Glue the playing directions to the front of the folder.

(Glue to oak tag. Color and cut out.)

Water Polo Spello

(Make two copies. Trim and glue to inside of file folder. Color and laminate.)
(Supply four white board markers and tissues.)

Water Polo Spello

ake	ame	ate
ape	ave	ade
ace	ale	are
ibe	ice	ipe
ile	ike	ime
ine	ite	ide
obe	ode	ole
one	ope	ose
ove	ome	oke
use	ure	uke
ume	ute	ube
ude	une	ule

(Glue to oak tag and cut apart.)

Neat Luggage

Vowel Teams: **ee, ea**

Two vowels together can make one vowel sound. The vowel teams **ee** and **ea** have the **long e** sound. The **ea** team can also have the **short e** sound. Read the **ee** and **ea** words.

Write the correct spelling for the word in each sentence.

I can swim in the _______________ end of the swimming pool.

deap deep dep

Patrick gave his pet hamster a _________________.

tret treet treat

We _____________________ jam and peanut butter on the bread.

spred spread spreed

Let's all_____________________ at my house at five o'clock.

meat meet met

I had a funny __________________ last night and woke up laughing.

dreme dream dreem

Tom can __________________ water for two minutes.

tread tred treed

Going Out of Town

17.

Vowel Teams: **ou, ow**

Two vowels together can make one vowel sound. The vowel teams **ou** and **ow** say the same vowel sound. The **w** in **ow** acts like a vowel. Read the **ou** and **ow** words.

Follow the directions.

Write the words that rhyme with **out.** __________ __________

Write the words that rhyme with **cow.** __________ __________

Add **ing** to **frown** and **clown.** __________ __________

Change the **p** in **pouch** to **c.** __________

Change the **m** in **mouth** to **s.** __________

Circle the two words in each sentence below that are not spelled correctly. Write the sentences with the correct spellings.

The klown painted a froun on his face.

____

____

The trowt opened his mowth to snap at the bait.

____

____

A Truckload

18.

Vowel Teams: **oa, ow, ai, ay**

Two vowels together can make one vowel sound. The vowel teams **oa** and **ow** say the **long o** sound. The vowel teams **ai** and **ay** say the **long a** sound. The letters **w** and **y** act like vowels. Read the **oa, ow, ai** and **ay** words.

Write the words that name the pictures.

________ ________ ________ ________

Write the rest of the words in the sentences below.

Our big ________ tree fell during the storm.

I made an elephant out of ________.

When I was sick, I had breakfast on a ________ in bed.

My ________ is missing a button.

My grandmother can ________ rugs from rags.

Tim helped his neighbor ________ his grass.

Hear that wind ________ through the trees!

The four o'clock ________ was ten minutes late.

A Cool Castle

19.

Vowel Teams: **oo moon, oo book**

The vowel team **oo** has two vowel sounds as in m**oo**n and b**oo**k.
Read the **oo** words.

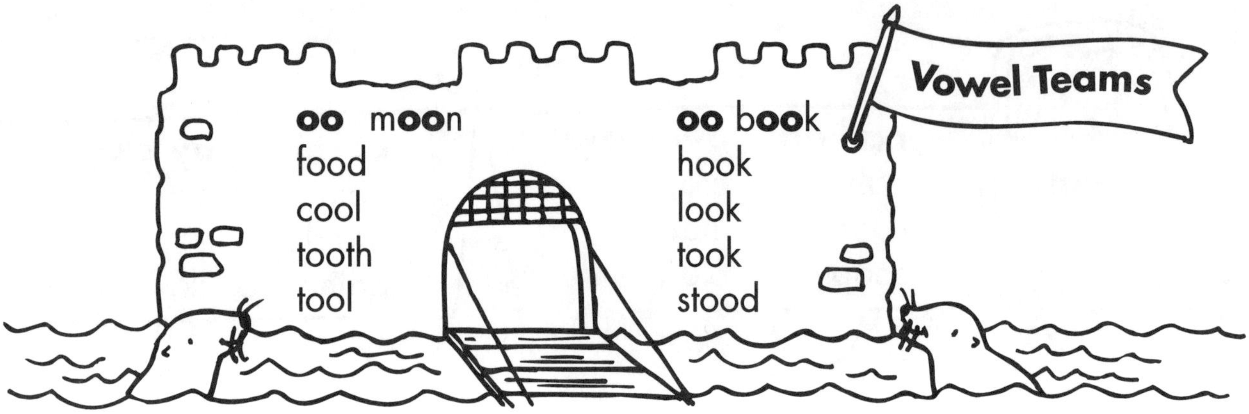

Fill in the Crossword Puzzle. Read the clues. Write the word that matches each clue by its number on the puzzle, going down or across.

Across

1. opposite of gave
3. something bent on which you hang things
4. something you eat to stay alive
6. not hot

Down

2. something used for biting and chewing
5. to see with the eyes
7. opposite of sat
8. handy thing to use to do work

Underwater Crew

Vowel Teams: **ew new, ew flew**

Sometimes vowel teams can be spelled the same way but have different sounds. The **ew** team can say the **long u** sound as in n**ew.** It can also say **oo** as in fl**ew.** The **w** in **ew** acts like a vowel. Read the **ew** words.

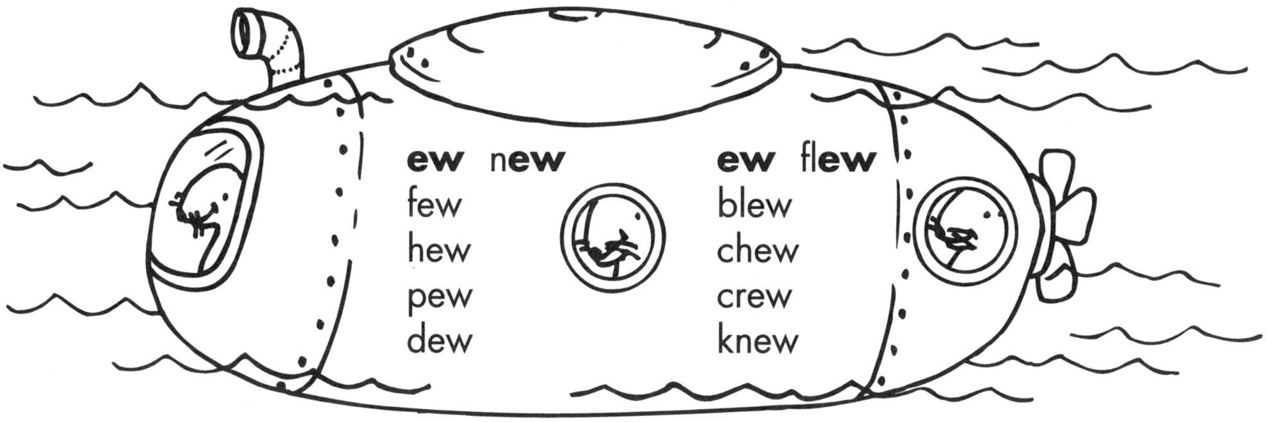

The letters of the words above have been scrambled in the following sentences. Read each sentence. Circle the scrambled word. Write its correct spelling on the line.

There were just a ewf rainy days this month. ____________

The grass was wet with wed. ____________

The wind welb the man's hat away. ____________

We are not allowed to wech gum in class. ____________

My family and I sat on the hard ewp in church.

____

The werc brought the ship safely back to the harbor.

____

I wekn that it was going to rain today. ____________

The men will whe the tree down for timber. ____________

What a Haul!

21.

Vowel Teams: **au, aw**

The vowel teams **au** and **aw** say the same sound as in P**au**l and s**aw.** They are not spelled the same. The **w** acts like a vowel. Read the **au** and **aw** words.

Find the **au** and the **aw** words in the Word Search Puzzle. Circle them. You can go across or down. One has been done for you.

v	b	j	h	a	u	l	c	e	m	q	u
g	w	d	a	k	f	a	i	a	d	t	y
x	s	l	u	r	n	u	s	h	r	a	w
f	a	w	n	p	z	n	a	p	a	m	b
c	u	o	t	d	f	c	r	a	w	l	n
e	l	g	l	h	i	h	j	k	o	p	s

On a Joy Ride

Vowel Teams: **oi, oy**

The vowel teams **oi** and **oy** say the same sound as in **oi**l and b**oy.** They are not spelled the same. The **y** in **oy** acts like a vowel. Read the **oi** and **oy** words.

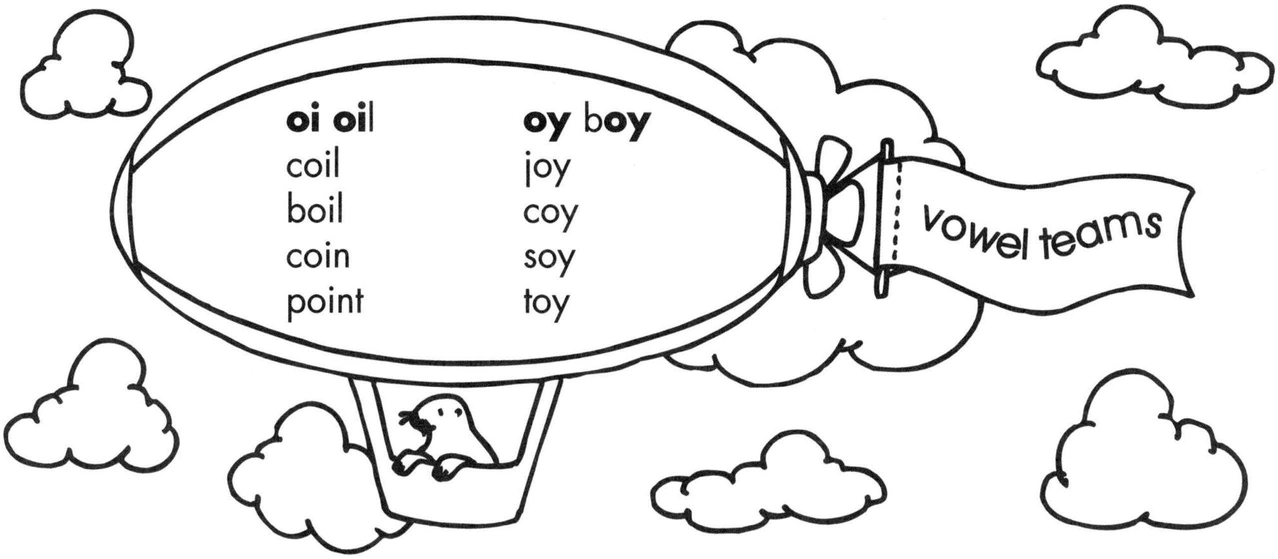

Make your own Word Search Puzzle for the words. Write the letters of each word next to each other in the squares. You can make the words go across or down. Fill in the rest of the squares with other letters. See if a friend can find and circle the words in your puzzle.

My Word Search

Vowel Team Round-up

Vowel Teams: **ee, ea, ou, ow, ai, oo, oa, ew, au, aw, oi, oy**

To Play:

Two can play. Each player takes a game board, a Vowel Team Spelling Sheet, a list of words, a narrow-tip white board felt marker, and a tissue. To start, a player gives a word from his/her word list to the other player to spell. The other player writes it on his/her Vowel Team Spelling Sheet. If correct, the player writes the vowel team in the word in the first circle after Start on his/her game board. If not, the player wipes off the incorrect word on the spelling sheet and gives the other player a word to spell. The first player to fill in all the circles with a vowel team from the round-up wins. Players check off the words used with the marker. Players check each other on their spelling. Wipe off the game at the end of play.

To Make:

Duplicate the game board and the Vowel Team Spelling Sheet two times. Make one copy of the word lists. Glue all to oak tag and laminate. Cut apart. Provide two narrow-tip white board felt markers and two tissues. Enclose all in a clasp envelope. Glue the playing directions to the front of the envelope.

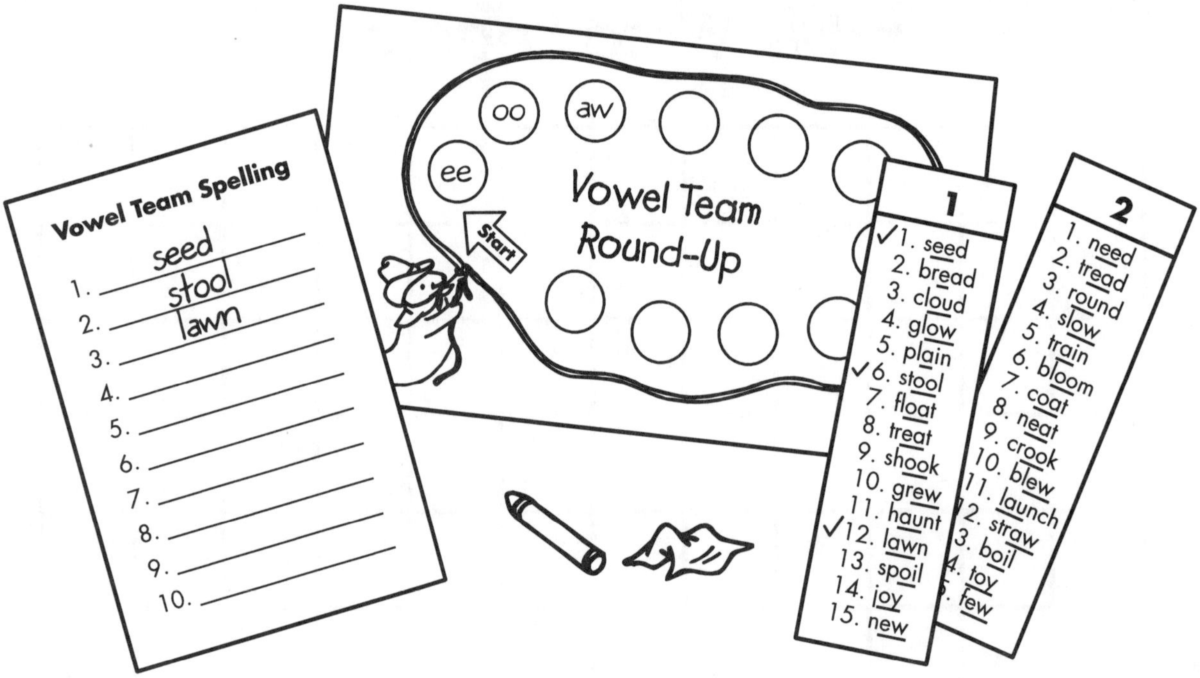

Vowel Team Round-up

(Make two copies of the game board. Laminate.)

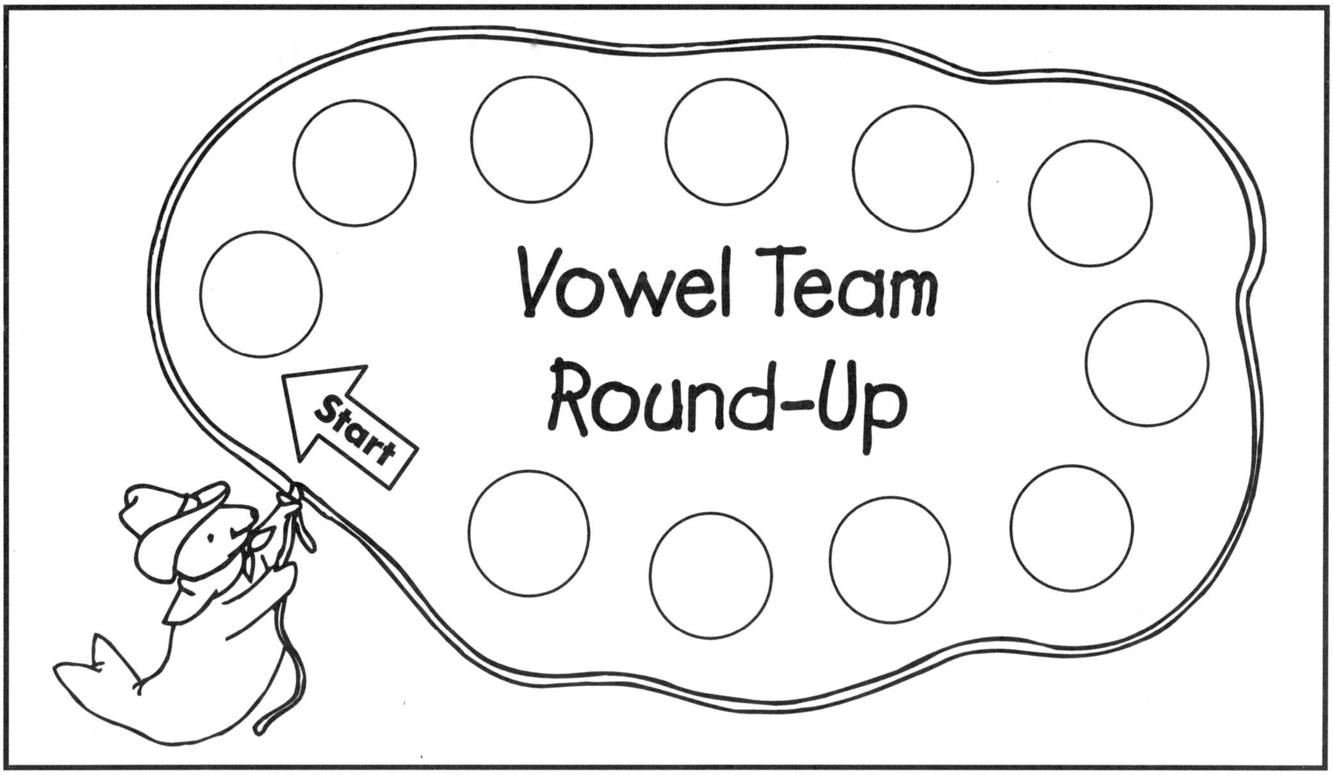

Vowel Team Spelling Sheet

1. ____________________
2. ____________________
3. ____________________
4. ____________________
5. ____________________
6. ____________________
7. ____________________
8. ____________________
9. ____________________
10. ____________________

(Make two copies of the Vowel Team Spelling Sheet. Laminate.)

(Make one copy of the word lists. Laminate.)

1	2
1. seed	1. need
2. bread	2. tread
3. cloud	3. round
4. glow	4. slow
5. plain	5. train
6. stool	6. bloom
7. float	7. coat
8. treat	8. neat
9. shook	9. crook
10. grew	10. blew
11. haunt	11. launch
12. lawn	12. straw
13. spoil	13. boil
14. joy	14. toy
15. new	15. few

Sound-Alikes

24.

R-controlled Vowels: **er, ir, ur**

A vowel is followed by **r in an r-controlled vowel.** The **r** controls the sound of the vowel. The **r-**controlled vowels **er**, **ir**, and **ur** say the same sound as in h**er**, b**ir**d, and f**ur.** They are not spelled the same. Read the **er, ir, and ur** words.

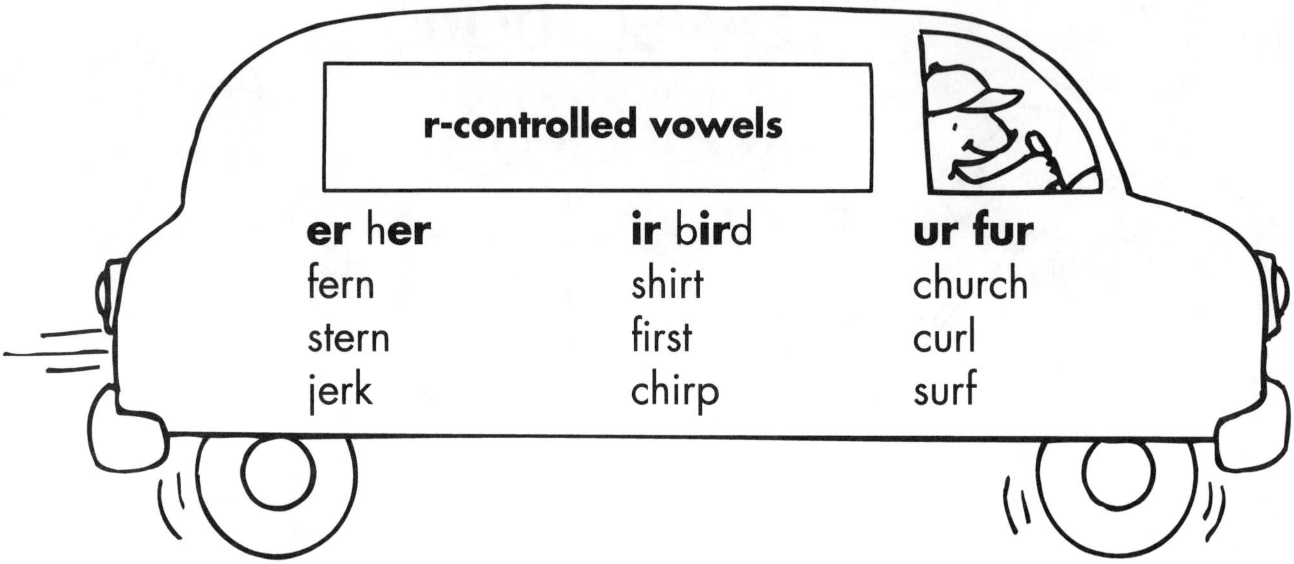

Write the word that matches the meaning.

a green, leafy plant ____________________

a tight ringlet ____________________

something you put on with a skirt or pants ________________

a noise a bird makes ____________________

a strict manner ____________________

to ride the waves on a board ____________________

to give a hard tug ____________________

comes before second ____________________

a place where you can pray ____________________

Racing Car

25.

R-controlled Vowels: **ar, or**

A vowel is followed by **r** in an **r-controlled vowel.** The **r** controls the sound of the vowel. The **r-controlled vowels ar** and **or** sound like **ar** as in st**ar** and **or** as in c**or**n. Read the **ar** and **or** words.

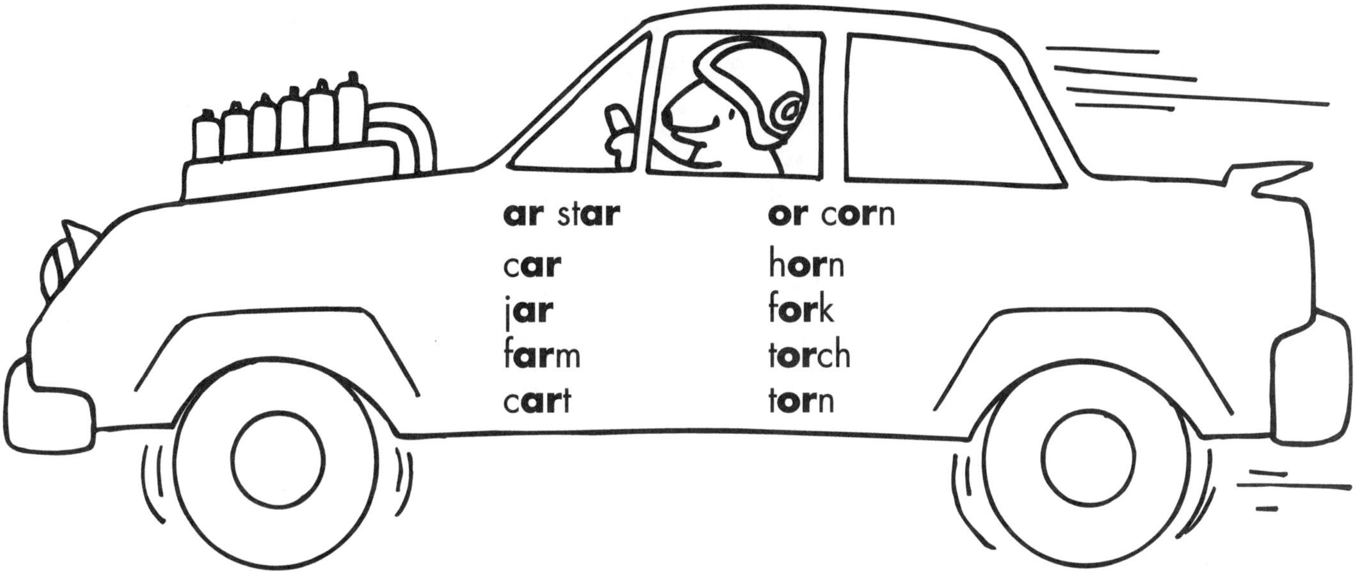

Write the correct **ar** or **or** word in each sentence.

We filled the ____________________ with food for the picnic.

Will you open this ____________________ for me?

I used my knife and ____________________ to cut the meat.

A thorn had ________________ a hole in my pocket.

Mom and Dad just bought a shiny new ________________.

My sister plays the French ____________ in the school band.

A ________________ lighted our path through the dark cave.

John spends the summer at his grandpa's ________________ in Iowa.

Farmer's Market

Farmer's Market

R-controlled Vowels: **ar, er, ir, or, ur**

To Play:

Two can play. Each player takes a Farmer's Market game board, a set of numbers (1–15), a word list, a white board marker, and a tissue. Players place their numbers face down in separate piles in their playing area. The first player takes a number from his/her number pile and reads it out loud. The second player reads the word from his/her word list for that number. The first player spells and writes the word on the game board under the matching r-controlled vowel pattern. If correctly spelled, the player leaves the word on the game board and discards the number. If not, the misspelled word must be wiped off with a tissue. The second player takes his/her turn. The player who fills in all the spaces under the ar, er, ir, or, and ur patterns first is the winner. If all the spaces for a pattern are filled, the player discards the number and loses a turn. Players check each other's spelling. Wipe off the game board to start another game. Players may trade word lists.

To Make:

Duplicate the game board and the number set two times. Duplicate the word lists once. Glue all to oak tag. Color if desired. Cut out the game board and laminate for a writing surface. Cut out the number sets. Place each set of numbers in zip-lock bag. Cut out the word lists. Slip one list into each zip-lock bag. Provide two narrow-tip white board markers and two tissues. Enclose all in a clasp envelope. Glue the playing directions to the front of the envelope.

Farmer's Market

(Duplicate the game board two times. Glue to oak tag. Laminate and cut out.)

ar	er	ir	or	ur

1	6	11
2	7	12
3	8	13
4	9	14
5	10	15

(Duplicate two times. Glue to oak tag and cut out.)

(Glue to oak tag and cut apart.)

1	2
1. car	1. far
2. her	2. fern
3. first	3. firm
4. corn	4. horn
5. turn	5. fur
6. park	6. mark
7. perk	7. perm
8. shirt	8. skirt
9. torn	9. born
10. churn	10. burp
11. sharp	11. shark
12. herd	12. perch
13. whirl	13. chirp
14. fork	14. cork
15. burn	15. hurt

Making Cupcakes

Compound Words

Two or more words can be put together to make compound words. The words **cup** and **cake** make the compound word **cupcake**. Make more compound words by putting words together.

cup + cake = cupcake

Write the compound word for each set of words. Draw a line to the picture.

hat + box ____________________ •

base + ball ____________________ •

nut + shell ____________________ •

pig + pen ____________________ •

pan + cake ____________________ •

bee + hive ____________________ •

Up the Flagpole

Compound Words

28.

Make compound words by putting two or more words together.

Draw a line between two words to make a compound word.

flag	box
hill	set
sand	bone
sun	cube
wish	pole
flash	top

Write the compound words in the sentences below.

We ran all the way to the _______________.

We could see a beautiful _______________.

Let's make a wish with the _______________.

We pulled the flag to the top of the ___________.

I lost my ring in the __________________.

We need a new _______________ for the camera.

Compound Blastoff 29.

Compound Blastoff

Compound Words Game

To Play:

Two can play. Spread the word cards face down on the playing area in rows. Each player takes a Compound Blastoff rocket, a tissue, and a white board marker. Each player in turn takes two word cards and turns them over. If the two cards make a compound word, the player writes the word on his/her rocket with the marker and discards the cards. If a compound can't be made, the cards are put back. The winner is the first player to have six compound words on his/her rocket. Players may refer to the Compound Word List to check on compound words. At the end of play, wipe off the rockets with the tissue.

To Make:

Duplicate the game setup. Glue rockets, word cards, and the word list to oak tag. Laminate the rockets and cut out. Cut out word cards. Enclose all in a clasp manila envelope with two white board markers and tissues. Glue the playing directions to the front of the envelope.

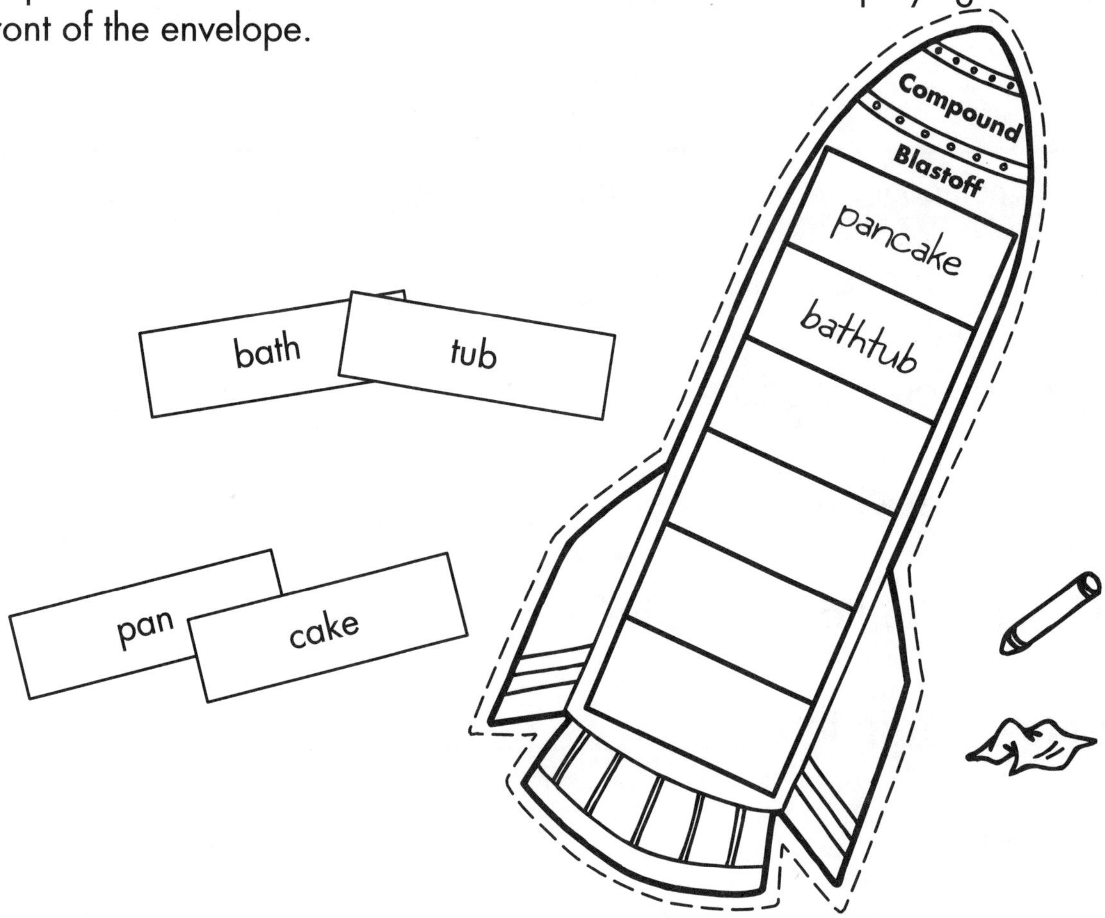

Compound Blastoff

(Glue to oak tag. Laminate and cut out. Provide white board markers and tissues.)

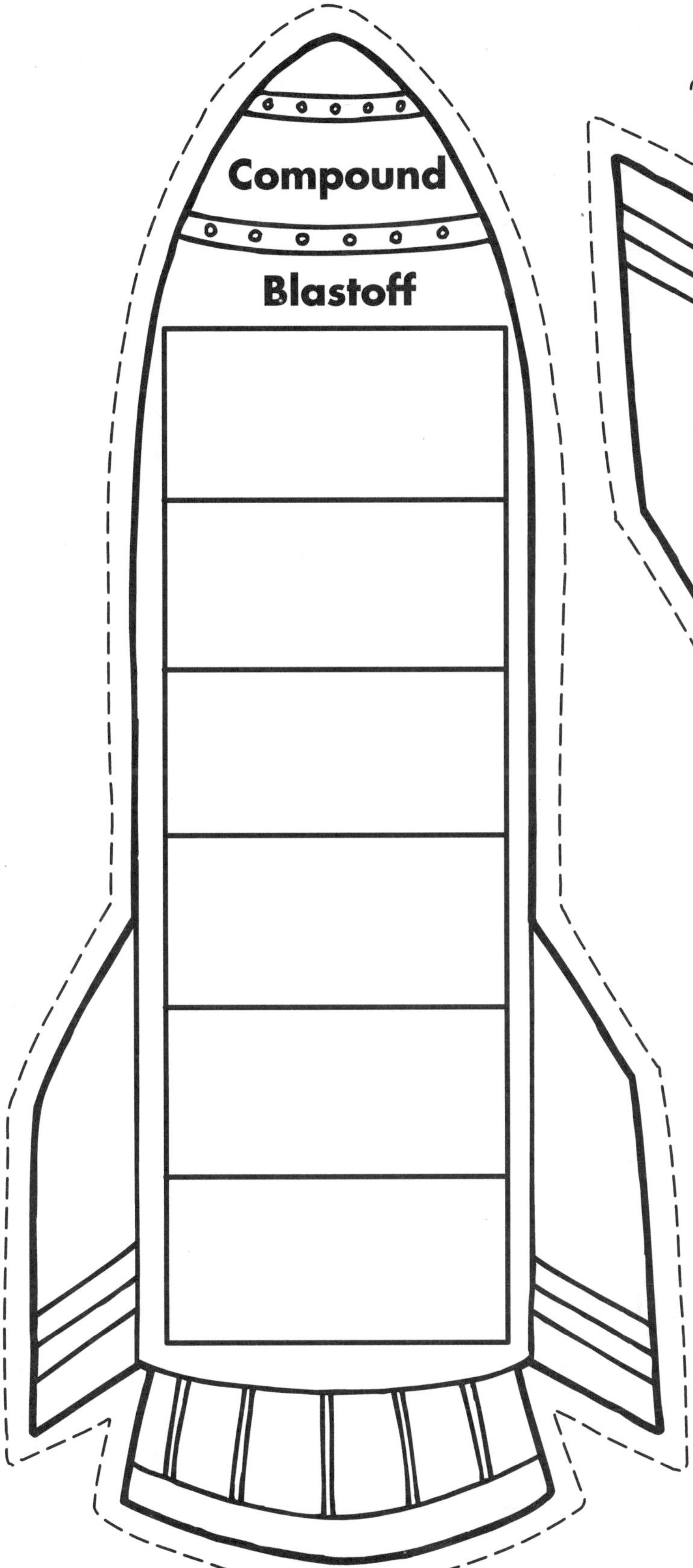

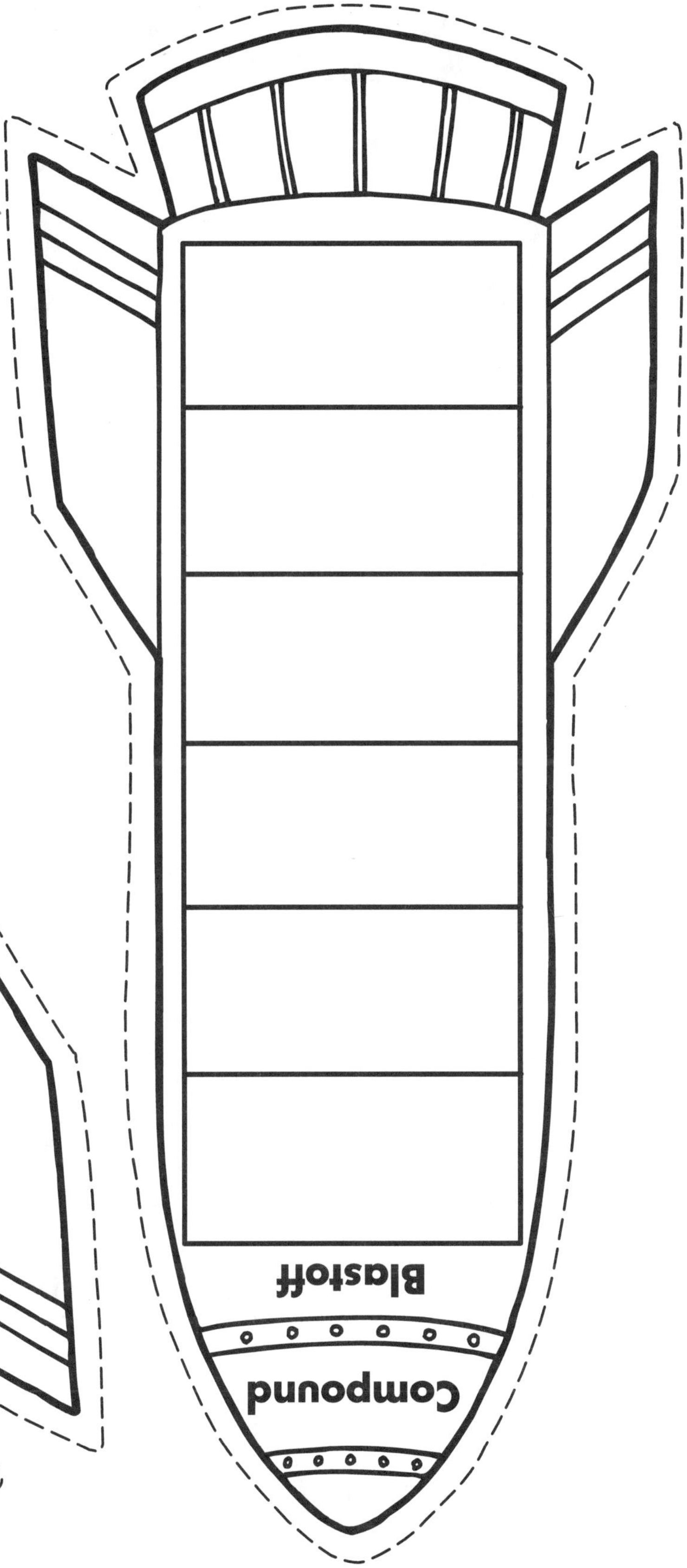

Compound Blastoff

cat	sand	pen
nip	box	pan
bat	flag	cake
man	pole	cup
hot	bath	cake
dog	tub	bath
sun	lime	robe
tan	pipe	hill
set	hat	side
shine	nut	wind
hill	shell	mill
top	pig	up

Compound Blastoff

set	class	space
sun	mate	ship
sling	dish	stove
shot	can	top
hand	ship	hand
shake	shape	trap
in	bed	fire
side	time	man
sun	can	wind
top	not	mill
gun	drug	rag
fish	store	bag

Compound Blastoff

rail	foot	meal
road	step	meat
cow	bee	ball
boy	hive	to
rain	bed	beam
bow	room	way
moon	team	storm
light	snow	back
barn	flake	bone
yard	pay	base
short	day	week
cut	oat	end

Compound Word List*

backbone
backfire
backyard
barnyard
baseball
bathroom
bathrobe
bathtub
batman
bedroom
bedside
beehive
cannot
catfish
catnip
classmate
classroom
cowboy
cupcake

dishpan
drugstore
flagpole
fireman
firetrap
football
footstep
gunshot
handbag
handgun
handshake
hilltop
hot-dog
inmate
inside
into
limestone
mealtime
meatball

moonbeam
moonlight
nutshell
oatmeal
pancake
payday
pigpen
ragbag
railroad
railway
rainbow
rainstorm
roommate
sandman
sandstone
sandstorm
setup
shipshape
shortcut

sit-up
slingshot
snowflake
snowman
snowstorm
spaceship
stovetop
sunlight
sunset
sunshine
suntan
teammate
today
upset
wayside
weekday
weekend
windmill
windpipe

*There may be more compound words than are listed. Check with the dictionary or the teacher.

(Glue to oak tag and cut.)

Puppet Show

30.

Syllables

A **syllable** has **one vowel sound.** It can be a **word** or **part** of a word with one vowel sound.

pup

puppet

Name the pictures below. Listen to how many **vowel sounds** you hear. Write the number of syllables.

 ______  ______  ______

 ______  ______  ______

Read each word below. Listen to how many **vowel sounds** you hear. Write the number of syllables.

cat ______ meet ______ handy______

butterfly______ no ______ basket ______

spoon ______ sunset ______ pail ______

treat ______ hammer______ December______

Tennis Match

31.

Syllables: **Dividing Between Two Consonants**

When a word has **2 consonants** between 2 vowels, **divide the word** between the 2 consonants.

Draw a line **between the 2 consonants** in each word.
Write the word in syllables. The first one has been done.

gal/lop gal - lop tennis_____-_____

mitten_____-_____ muffin_____-_____

trumpet_____-_____ bandit_____-_____

basket_____-_____ mascot_____-_____

Robots on Parade

Syllables: **Dividing After the First Vowel**

When a word has **1 consonant** between **2 vowels,** divide **after the first vowel.** The first vowel will say its name.

Draw a line **after the first vowel** in each word. The first vowel will say its name. Write the word in syllables. The first one has been done.

mu|sic mu - sic

tulip____ - ____

vacant____ - ____

robot____ - ____

totem____ - ____

minus____ - ____

pupil____ - ____

silent____ - ____

Toss the Salad

Syllables: **Dividing After the Consonant**

When a word has **1 consonant** between **2 vowels,** the word can be divided **after the consonant.** The first vowel will have the short sound.

Draw a line **after the consonant** in each word. The first vowel will have the short sound. Write the word in syllables. The first one has been done.

lem/on lem - on   linen ____-____

salad ____-____   tenant ____-____

prison ____-____   solid ____-____

canon ____-____   dragon ____-____

Surfing Along

Spelling by Syllables

Spell longer words by breaking them into syllables.
Remember the syllable division patterns below.

Divide between the consonants	Divide after the vowel	Divide after the consonant

Divide the words into syllables by drawing a line. Write the words by syllables. The first one has been done.

button   but - ton

salad   ________ - ________

robot   ________ - ________

trumpet   ________ - ________

melon   ________ - ________

totem   ________ - ________

basket   ________ - ________

remember   ________ - ________ - ________

potato   ________ - ________ - ________

Taking Root

The Base Word

> A **base** word is the **main** word. Other words can be made using a base word.

Circle the base word in each word.

(camp)ing	skated	childish
uncut	retie	mistook

Write the base word for each word.

bending bend ____________ sunny ____________

fried ____________ pennies ____________

coats ____________ ripped ____________

finest ____________ dreamer ____________

Make more words by adding each ending to the base word.

sand sander ____________ ____________ ____________

er ing ed

rich ____________ ____________ ____________

es er est

Replay It!

36.

Prefixes: **un-, dis-, re-**

A **prefix** comes **before** a base word. A prefix adds to the meaning of the word. Read the prefixes and their meanings.

un- = not, the opposite of **dis-** = not, the opposite of **re-** = again

Add the correct prefix to the base word to finish each sentence.

We need to ______load the groceries from the car.

un- dis- re-

Don't forget to ______turn your books to the library.

un- dis- re-

I ______like going to the dentist.

un- dis- re-

Read each meaning. Add the correct prefix to the underlined base word. Write the new word.

to make again ____________________

re- dis-

not fair ____________________

re- un-

the opposite of color ____________________

dis- re-

Preheat It!

37.

Prefixes: **in-, mis-, pre-**

A **prefix** comes **before** a base word. A prefix adds to the meaning of the word. Read the prefixes and their meanings.

in- = in, into, not **mis-** = wrongly, badly **pre-** = before

Add the correct prefix to the base word to finish each sentence.

My mother must ______cook the dinner for the party.

in- mis- pre-

We have to play ______doors when it rains.

in- mis- pre-

I made a big ______take on my test.

in- mis- pre-

Read each meaning. Add the correct prefix to the underlined base word. Write the new word.

the side that is in ______________________

in- pre-

to spell wrongly ______________________

pre- mis-

to test before ______________________

pre- in-

Resting Seal

Suffixes: **-ing, -ed, -less**

A **suffix** comes **after** a base word. A suffix adds to the meaning of the word. Read the suffixes and their meanings.

-ing = doing something   **-ed** = did something in the past   **-less** = without

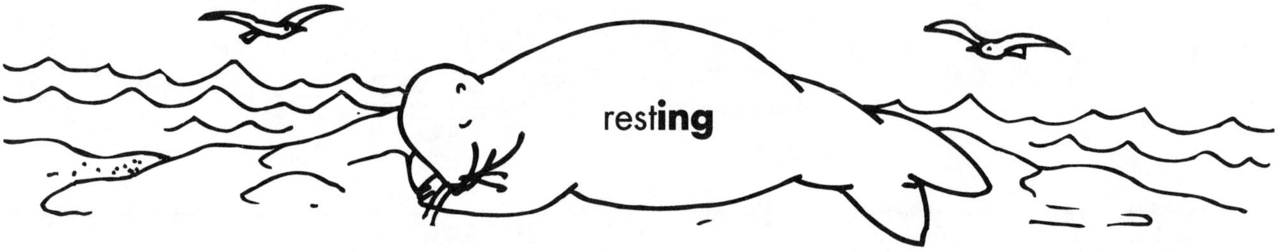

Circle the suffixes **-ing, -ed,** and **-less** in the words. Read each word.

dent(ed)	running	careless
farming	hopeless	fainted
tanned	resting	harmless
loading	helpless	rusted

Write **-ing, -ed,** or **-less** to complete the words in the sentences.

The thin and hungry dog looked friend____________.

We roast_________ marshmallows and hot dogs at camp.

The boys enjoyed sleep___________ in the cabin loft.

Super Catcher

Suffixes: **-er, -ly, -y**

A **suffix** comes **after** the base word. A suffix adds to the meaning of the word. Read the suffixes and their meanings.

-er = the person or thing that does something

-ly = like

-y = full of

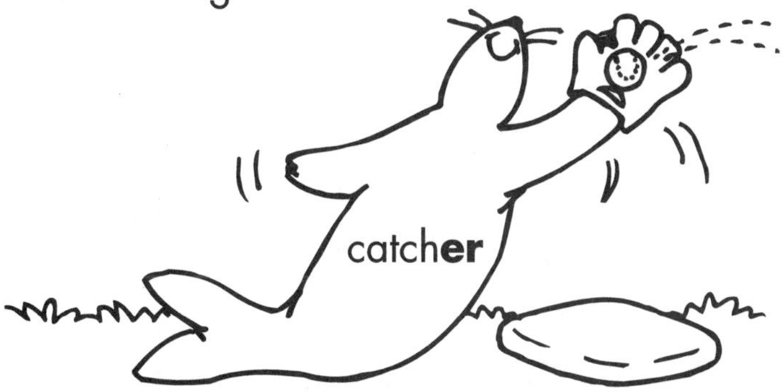

Circle the suffixes **-er, -ly,** and **-y** in the words. Read each word.

roomy	hardly	skinny
coaster	sunny	winner
lovely	pesky	thinker
batter	badly	rocky

Write **-er, -ly,** or **-y** to complete the words in the sentences.

We bare______________ had time to catch the plane.

The pitch_____________ threw the ball high and fast.

The attic is a room____________ place to store things.

Reachable Apple

40.

Suffixes: **-able, -ish, -ful**

A **suffix** comes **after** a base word. A suffix adds to the meaning of the word. Read the suffixes and their meanings.

-able = able to, can   **-ish** = like, somewhat   **-ful** = full of

Circle the suffixes -**able**, -**ish**, and -**ful** in the words. Read each word.

teach(able)	boyish	careful
playful	passable	girlish
blackish	harmful	readable
trainable	babyish	cheerful

Write **-able, -ish,** or **-ful to complete the words in the sentences.**

Our vacation at the ranch was rest_______________.

We took our port____________ radio to the beach.

Bill played the part of the fool___________ lad in the play.

Pitch the Ball

Spelling Rules: **The ck, tch Rule**

Write **ck** or **tch** after one **short vowel** as in Ja**ck** and pi**tch.**

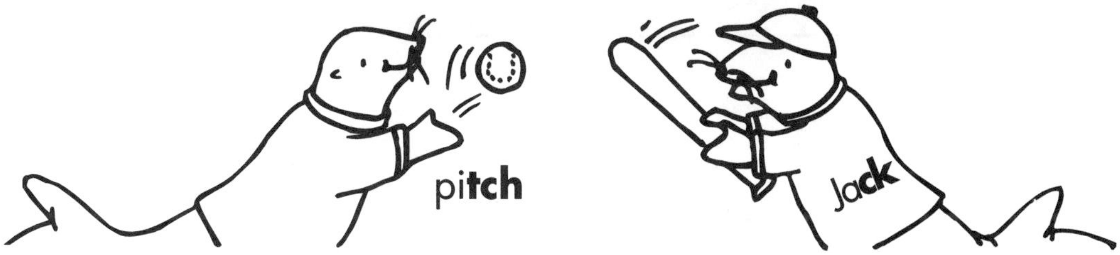

Write the correct **ck** or **tch** word in each sentence.

Jim likes to play ____________________ with his friends.

fetch hutch catch

I found a very smooth ____________________ at the beach.

rock lick deck

My cat was ____________________ all week but is better now.

luck sick tack

Mom and I made a ____________________ of cookies.

botch match batch

The play went on without a ____________________ .

patch hitch hutch

Will you ____________________ me into bed?

tuck buck back

John won the tennis ____________________ yesterday.

pitch match witch

I need to ____________________ my bag for the trip.

pick pack buck

Toss the Ball

42.

Spelling Rules: **The f, l, s, z Rule**

Double the **f, l, s,** or **z after one vowel** as in pu**ff**, be**ll**, bo**ss**, and bu**zz.** Some exceptions are **bus, gas, if,** and **pal.**

Read the words. Write an **ff, ll, ss,** or **zz** word in each sentence.

huff	call	mess	buzz
stuff	fell	toss	jazz

Please ______________ me when you get home.

What a big ______________ we made in art class.

My dad likes _______________ music.

Will you _________________ the ball to the dog?

I _____________ and hurt myself.

I will ____________ and puff and blow your house in!

Listen to those bees _____________ in the hive.

I like to ______________ things into my pockets.

Cats and Dogs

43.

Spelling Rules: **Plurals** with **-s**

For most **name** words, just **add s** to show more than one or the **plural form.**

Read the words. Add s to each word to show more than one or the **plural** form. Write the word.

parks ___parks___

book ________

tent ________

bee ________

coat ________

hand ________

train ________

Foxes in Boxes

44.

Spelling Rules: **Plurals** with **-es**

Add **-es** to words that end with **s, x, ch, sh,** or **tch** to show more than one or the **plural** form.

Add **-es** to these words that end with **s, x, ch, sh,** and **tch** to show more than one or the **plural** form.

glas**s**____

fo**x**____

pea**ch**____

di**sh**____

ma**tch**____

Add **-es** to these words that end with **s, x, ch, sh,** and **tch.** Write the words.

box ____________________

wish ____________________

bench ____________________

bus ____________________

witch ____________________

pass ____________________

Raking Leaves

Spelling Rules: **Plurals** for **-f** and **-fe** Words

For words that end with **f** or **fe,** change the **f** or **fe** to **ves** as in li**fe** to li**ves** and lea**f** to lea**ves.**

Read the words. Make them show more than one by crossing off the **f** or the **fe** and adding **ves.** Write the plural.

shel~~f~~ ves ____________

li~~fe~~ ves ____________

elf ____________

wife ____________

loaf ____________

knife ____________

wolf ____________

safe ____________

Shorten It!

Contractions

A contraction is made up of two words that are shortened. The two words are put together and a letter or letters is taken out. An apostrophe (') is written to take the place of the letter or letters. In the contraction **isn't,** the letter **o** was taken out from **not** in **is not.** Read the contractions below.

can't	won't
she'll	we'd
we're	it's
wasn't	don't
hadn't	I'll

Write the contraction for each pair of words that follows. Cross out the letters that were taken out. The first one is done.

can + ~~not~~ = can't

she + will = ______________

it + is = ____________________

had + not = ______________

was + not = ______________

we + are = _______________

we + would = ___________

I + will = _________________

do + not = _______________

will + not = ______________

Write the contraction for each pair of words in the sentences.

1. We ________________ go to the beach today.
(cannot)

2. I ________________ forget to meet you at noon.
(will not)

3. I am so glad that ________________ back in school.
(we are)

Own It!

47.

Possessives

Possessives are words that show ownership. To make a word show ownership, add an apostrophe (') and an **s.** Read the possessives below.

the seal**'s** pup

the boy**'s** truck

the girl**'s** dress

the boat**'s** sail

Write the possessive for each word below. The first one is done.

1. the gloves of the lady = lady**'s** glove
2. the hat the man owns = ______________
3. the game that belongs to Bob = ______________
4. the house of my friend = ______________
5. the park that the city owns = ______________

Write the possessive for the word below the blank in each sentence.

1. The ______________ ball rolled down the hill.
   boy
2. My ______________ tail wagged when he saw me.
   dog
3. ______________ hammer was in the tool chest.
   Dad
4. The ______________ park is near the library.
   city
5. The ______________ desk is near the window.
   teacher

Just Add the Apostrophe (')

48.

Possessives

Just add the apostrophe (′) for words that end with **s** or are **more than one.** See the possessives below.

the seals′ rock
the ants′ hill
the boss′ party
the teams′ coaches

Write the possessive for each word below. Just add the (′).
The first one is done.

1. the food of many dogs = dogs′ food
2. the fins of the fishes = ________________
3. the pages of the books = ________________
4. the bats that the teams own = ________________
5. the hive that belongs to the bees = ________________

Write the possessive for the word below the blank in each sentence.

1. The seven ________________ beds were lined up in a row.
   dwarfs
2. Three pairs of ________________ eyes glared at me.
   cats
3. The ________________ peels were cut into thin strips.
   oranges
4. The ________________ tracks were seen everywhere.
   animals
5. The funny ________________ acts were enjoyed by all.
   clowns

Double It!

The Doubling Rule: **Adding Suffixes**

For 1 syllable words
that end with 1 consonant
after 1 vowel
Double the **last consonant** when adding a **suffix** that **begins with a vowel.**

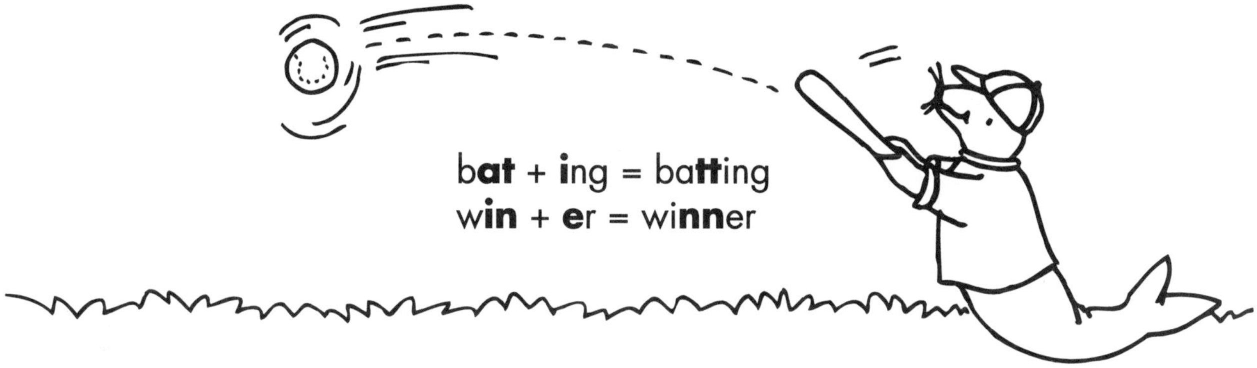

b**at** + **i**ng = ba**tt**ing
w**in** + **e**r = wi**nn**er

Just add suffixes that **begin with a consonant**, such as **l**ess, **f**ul, and **l**y.

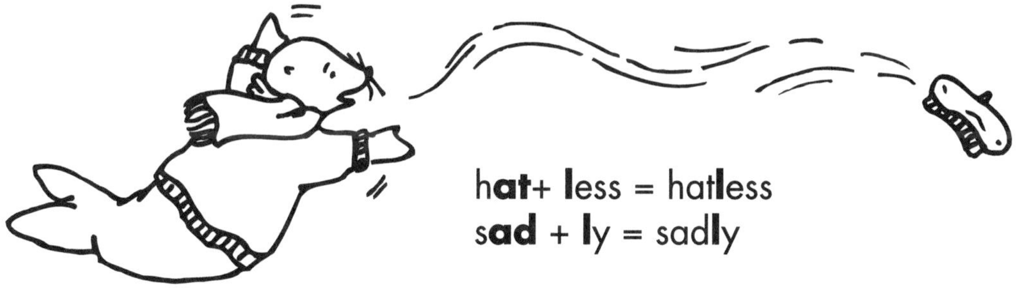

h**at**+ **l**ess = hat**l**ess
s**ad** + **l**y = sad**l**y

Double the last consonant of these 1-1-1 words and add the **vowel** suffix. Circle the double letters.

f**an** + **e**d fanned ________ z**ip** + **e**r ________

sk**ip** + **i**ng ________ b**et** + **i**ng ________

st**op**+ **e**r ________ s**un** + **e**d ________

Just add the consonant suffix to these 1-1-1 words.

gl**ad** + **l**y gladly ________ p**eg** + **l**ess ________

c**up** + **f**ul ________ b**ad** + **l**y ________

j**ob** + **l**ess________ b**ag**+ **f**ul ________

Drop It!

50.

The Final e Rule: **Adding Suffixes**

For words that end with **e,**
Drop the e to add a **suffix** that **begins with a vowel.**

hop~~e~~ + **i**ng = hoping
div~~e~~ + **e**d = dived

Just add suffixes that begin with a consonant, such as **l**ess, **f**ul, and **l**y.

shap**e** + **l**ess = shapeless
tim**e** + **l**y = timely

Drop the e of these final e words and add the **vowel** suffix.
Cross off the final e.

nam~~e~~ + ing naming ______ time + er ______

wipe + ed ______ rope + ing ______

rule + er ______ bake + ed ______

Just add the consonant suffix to these final e words.

hope + ful hopeful ______ tire + less ______

lone + ly ______ grate + ful ______

tune + less ______ fine + ly ______

Change It!

The Y Rule: **Adding Suffixes**

For a word that **ends** with **y after a consonant, <u>change</u>** the **<u>y</u>** to **<u>i</u>** and add **any** suffix **<u>except</u>** a suffix that begins with an **i.**

fry (y → i) + **e**d = fried

candy (y → i) + **e**s = candies

Just add suffixes that begin with an **i.**

spy + **i**ng = spying

copy + **i**ng = copying

<u>Change</u> <u>the **y** to **i**</u> and add the suffixes that do not begin with **i.**

cry (y → i) + es cries

spry + ly ________________

handy + est ________________

copy + ed ________________

dry +ed ________________

dry +er ________________

Just add the suffixes that begin with i.

copy + ing copying

dry + ish ________________

baby + ish ________________

carry + ing ________________

hurry + ing ________________

sandy + ish ________________

75 Most Commonly Misspelled Words

52.

again
all right
any
asked
because
been
children
come
could
dear
didn't
do
does
done
every
first
for
four
friend
from
getting
girl
goes
here
hole

how
knew
know
laugh
many
money
of
off
once
one
only
our
people
pretty
put
read
said
saw
school
should
some
something
sometimes
stopped
talk

than
their
then
there
they
they're
threw
through
too
two
use
very
walk
want
was
went
were
what
when
where
which
who
whole
would
you're

Study these words until you have mastered them.
Use the **Work Out!** form to study.

Work Out!

Study Your Words

1 Write the word. Name the letters and trace 3 times or more. Say the word.	**2** Copy the word. Name and trace 3 times or more. Say the word.	**3** **Test 1:** Cover the word. Write the word. If it is right, go on to the next word. If not, go back and study 1 and 2. Test again in number 4.	**4** **Test 2**

53.

The Big Juggling Act

Synonyms

54.

Synonyms are words that mean the same thing or about the same thing. The words **small** and **little** are synonyms.

Find the **synonym matches.** Cut out the words. Put them on the circles with the words that mean about the same thing.

sprint | grasp | drag | dash | pull | clutch

Shell Opposites

Antonyms

Antonyms are words that mean the opposite.
The words **up** and **down** are **antonyms.**

Find the **antonym matches** for the shells. Cut out the shells. Put them next to their **antonym matches.**

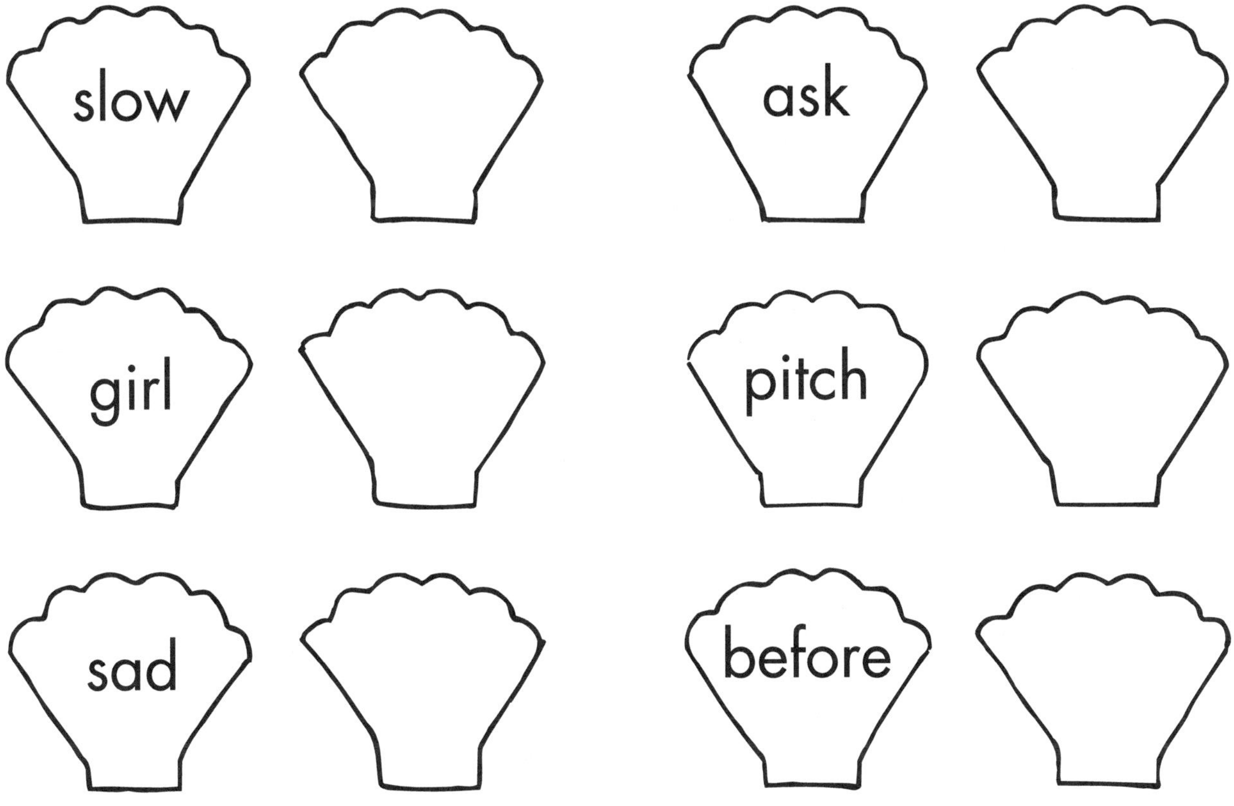

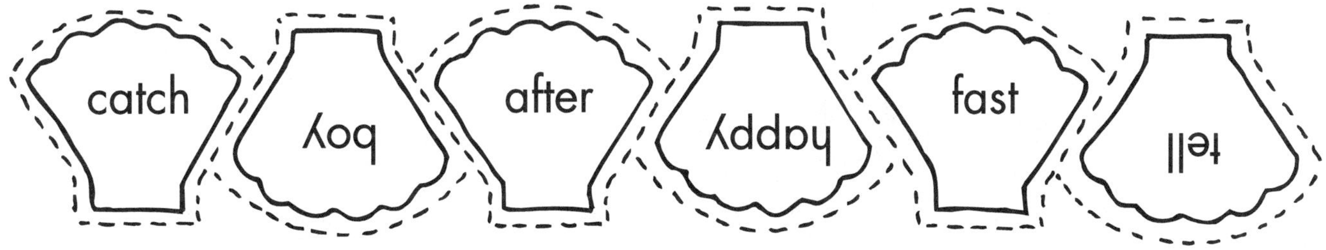

Piping Hot Loaves

Categories

Categories are **sets that are alike** in some way.

Name the **set** of things on each loaf. Cut out the labels. Put them on the matching loaves.

saw hammer
drill knife

football soccer
baseball golf

red blue
green orange

apples oranges
bananas lemons

cloudy rainy
sunny windy

Sports

Tools

Weather

Fruits

Colors

Sets and Lists

57.

Categories

Categories **are** sets that are alike **in some way.**

Write under each label the things that go together.

Foods

____
____
____
____

Drinks

____
____
____
____

Clothing

____
____
____
____

Round Things

____
____
____
____

rings	robe	pizza	dish	cocoa	spaghetti
moon	shirt	juice	ball	salad	soda
dress	steak	milk	pants		

Packing Factory

Categories

58.

Categories **are** sets that are alike **in some way.**

Cut out each list. Put each list into the box with its matching label.

cake	carpenter	hands	cobra
pies	teacher	feet	rattlesnake
ice cream	engineer	head	python
pudding	farmer	arms	boa constrictor

Layers of Meaning

A word can have different meanings.

Find the different meanings for each word on the cakes. Cut out the meanings. Put them on the cakes with the matching words.

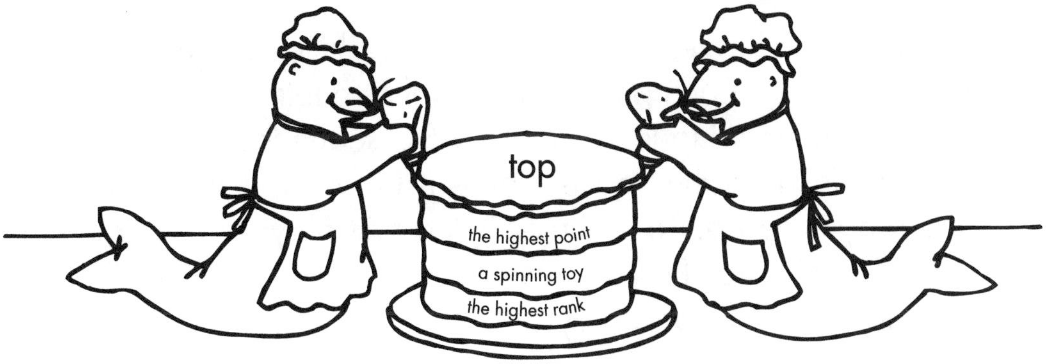

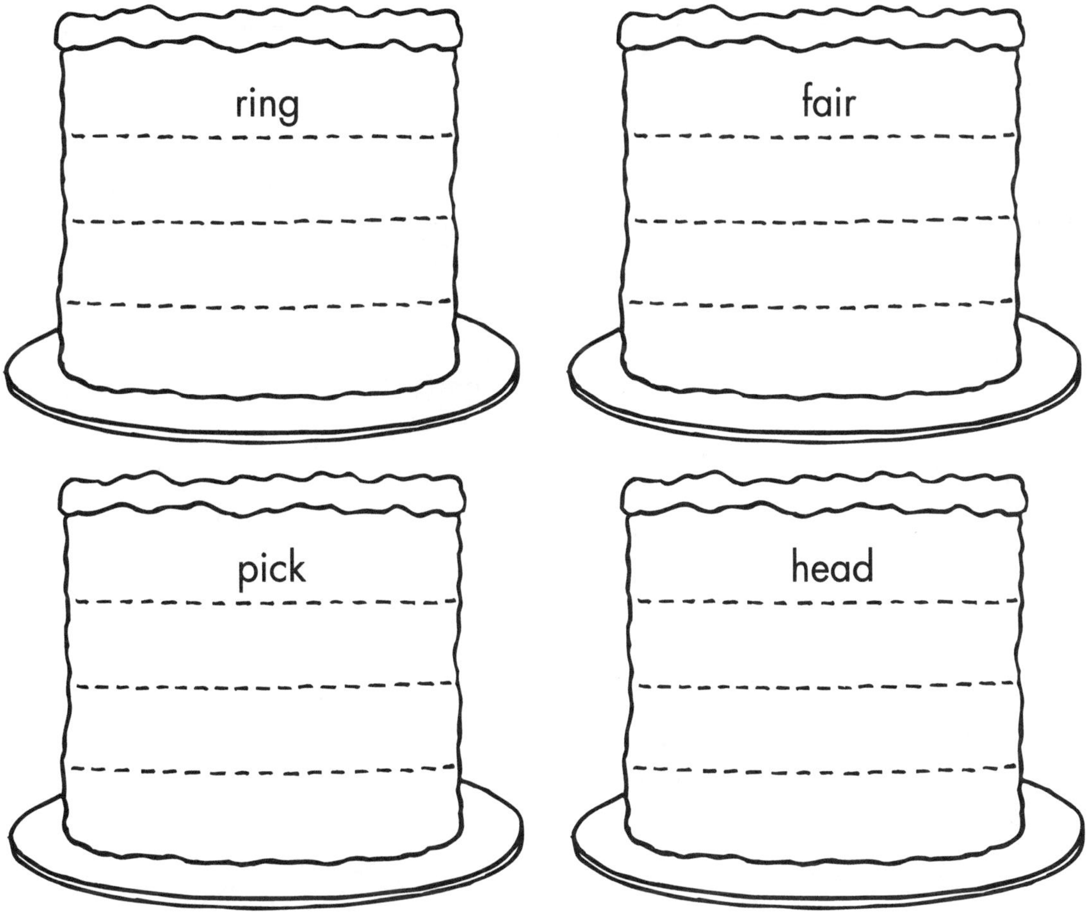

to pluck	a pointed tool for breaking soil, rock	to choose	sound of a bell
to be the leader	to form a circle	clear and sunny	to be just and honest
a band to wear on a finger	to go in a certain direction	pale, light skinned	part of body above the neck

ABC Sea Ships

Alphabetical Letter Sequence

To Play:

Three can play. Each player takes an ABC Sea Ship. Turn the clothespins face down in the playing area. Each player in turn takes a letter clothespin and checks to see if it is one of the missing letters in the ABC sequence on his/her Sea Ship. If it is, the player pins it to the space where it belongs. If not, the clothespin is returned to the playing area. The winner is the first player to pin all the missing letters on his/her Sea Ship. Play continues until all missing letters are pinned. Players may trade Sea Ships and play again.

To Make:

Glue ABC Sea Ships and clothespin letters to oak tag. Color and laminate if desired. Cut out. Glue letters to clothespins. Enclose all in a clasp manila envelope. Glue directions to the front of the envelope.

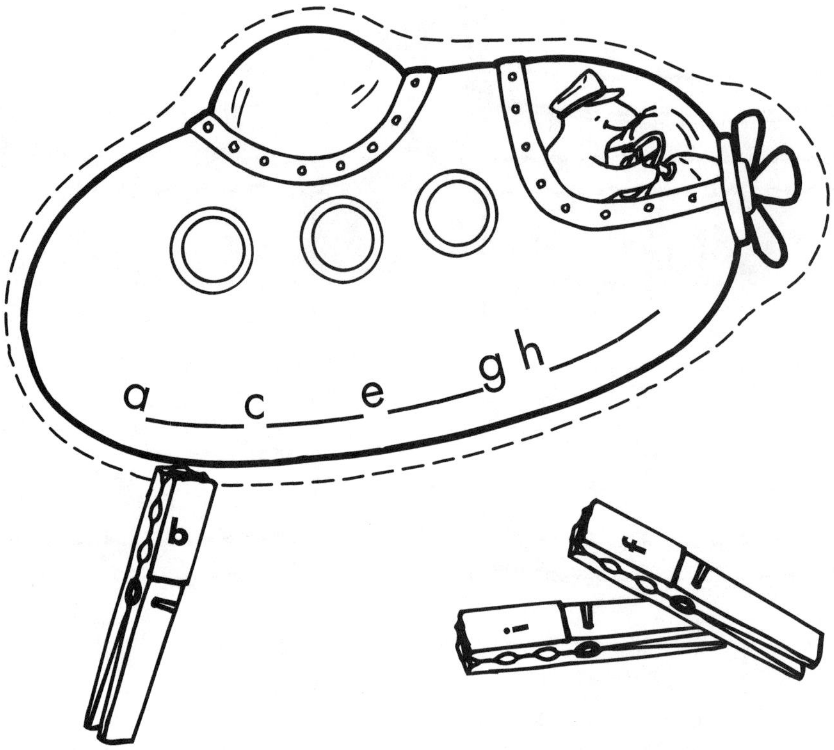

ABC Sea Ships

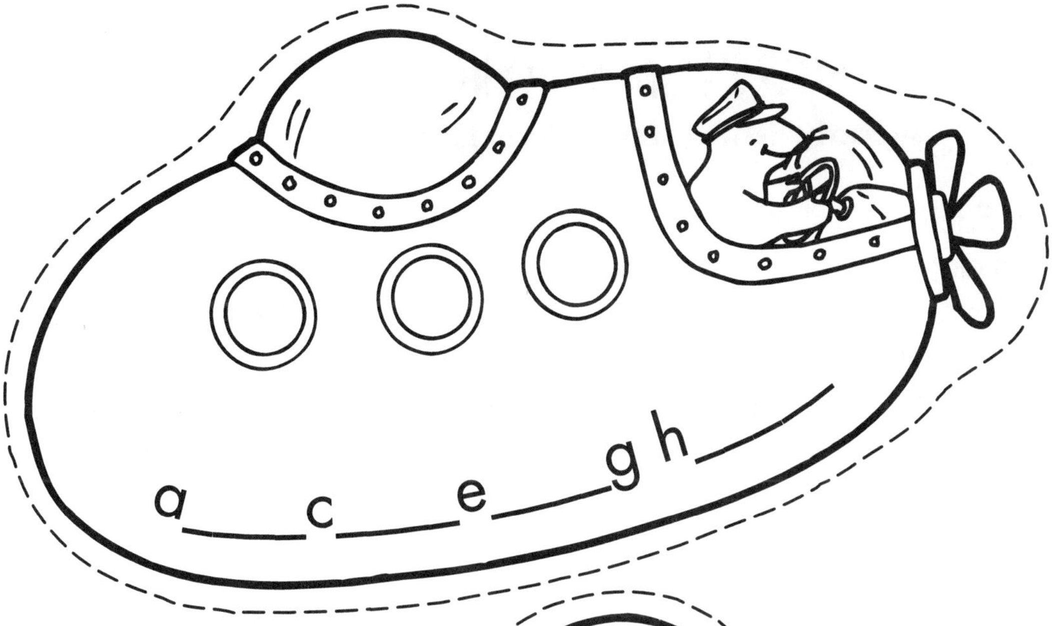

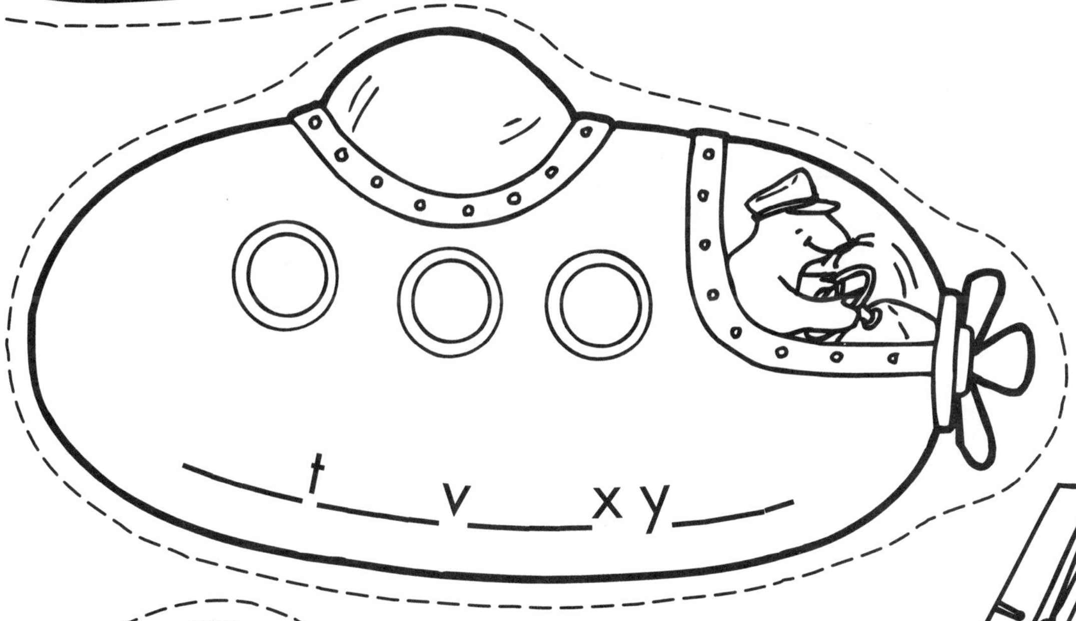

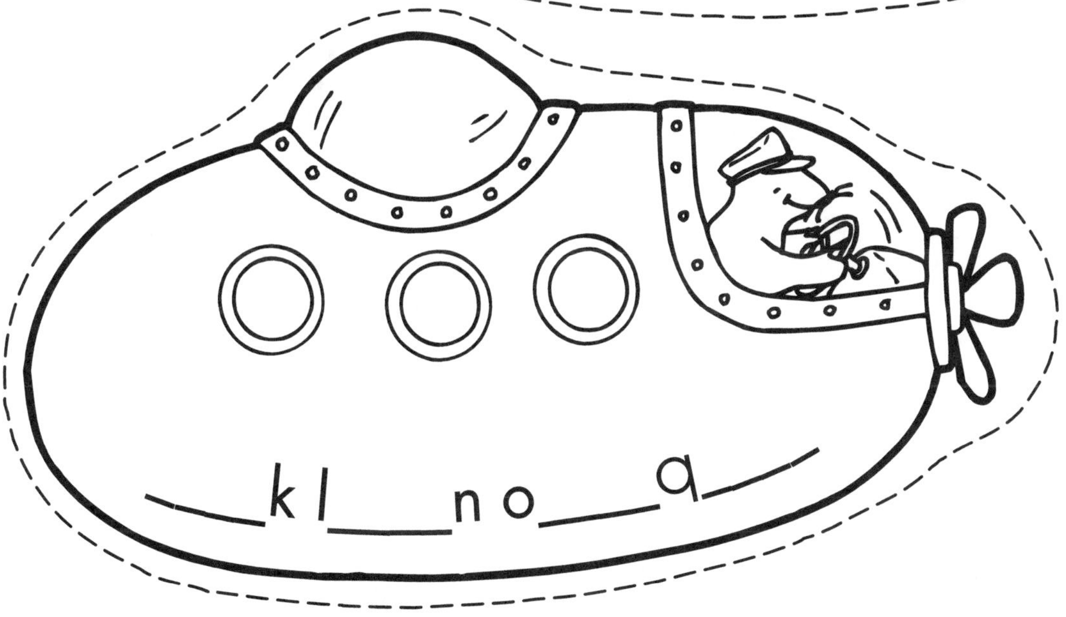

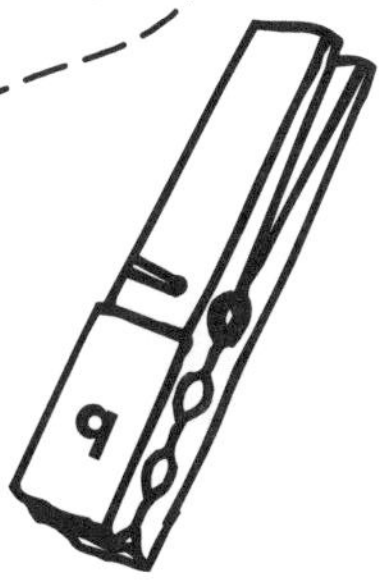

b	f	i	d
j	m	p	r
u	w	z	s

ABC Star Wheels

Alphabetical Order by First Letter

To Play:

Five may play. Each player takes a numbered star wheel, matching star sheet, and five numbered clothespins, 1–5. One player will get the six-pointed star wheel and take an additional clothespin for a challenge. Each player also takes a white board marker and a tissue. Players see who can be the first to pin their words in alphabetical order by the first letter. Players check each other's work for accuracy. If correct, players may write their words in alphabetical order on the laminated star sheets with the white board marker. Players check each other again for accuracy. Players may play another round of Star Wheels by exchanging wheels and star sheets. Wipe star sheets with a tissue to reuse.

To Make:

Glue star wheels, star sheets, and clothespin numbers to oak tag. Color. Laminate the star sheets. Cut out the wheels, star sheets, and clothespin numbers. Glue numbers to clothespins. Supply five white board markers. Store all in a clasp manila envelope. Glue the playing directions to the front of the envelope.

ABC Star Wheels

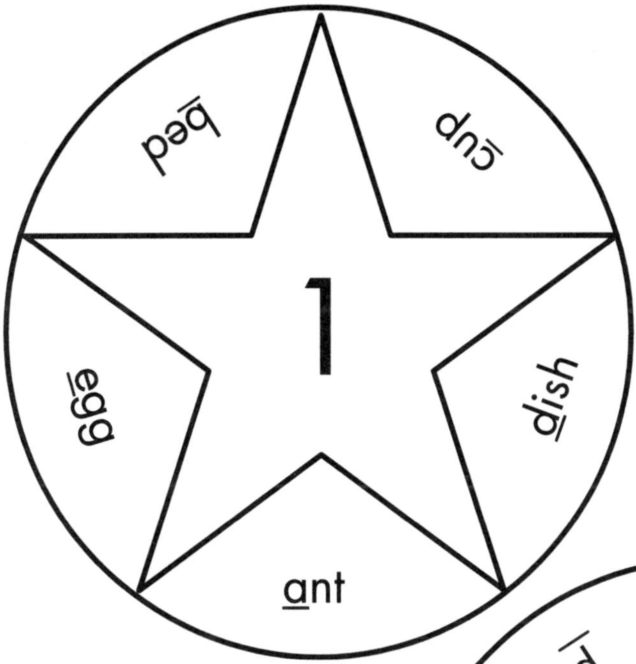

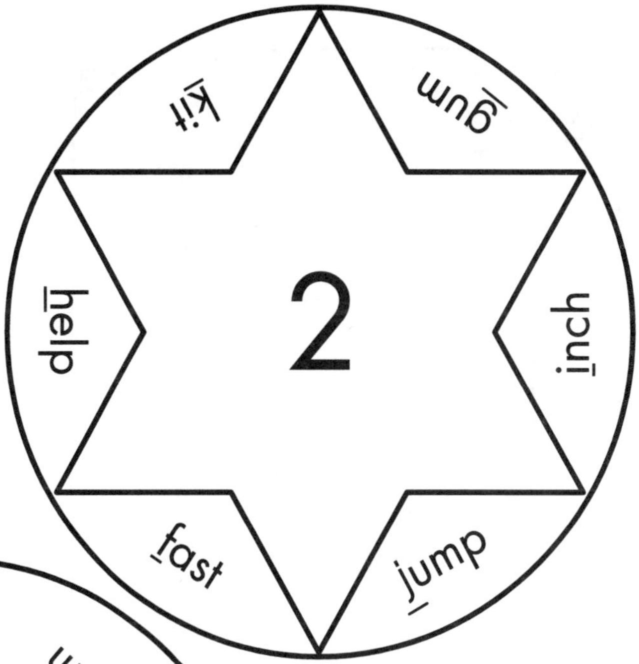

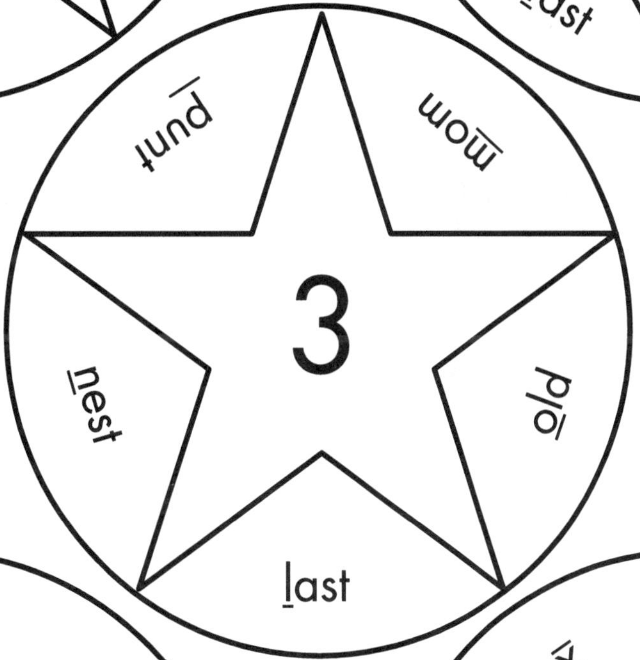

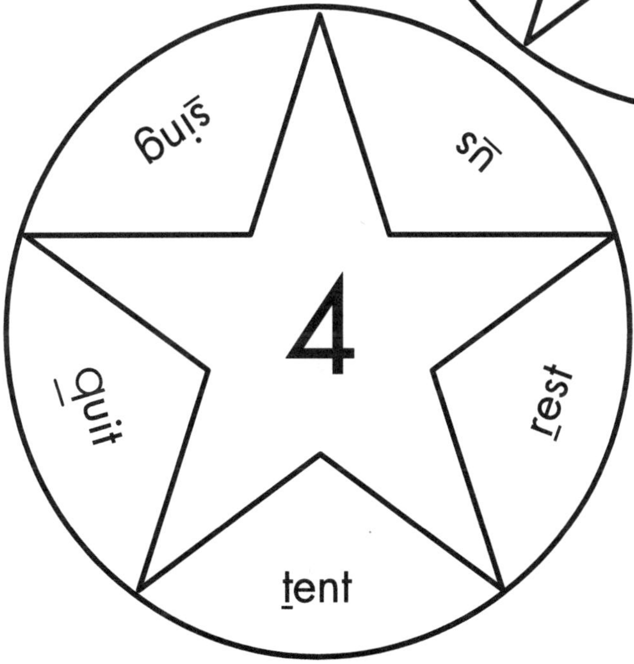

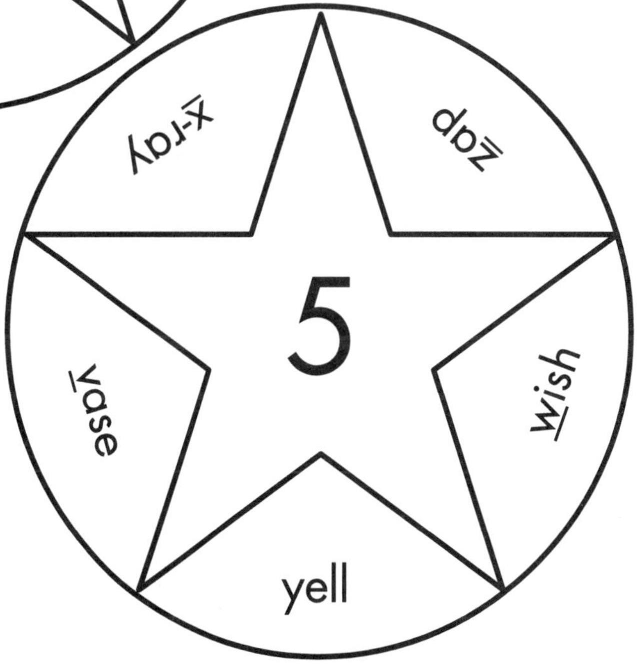

ABC Star Wheels

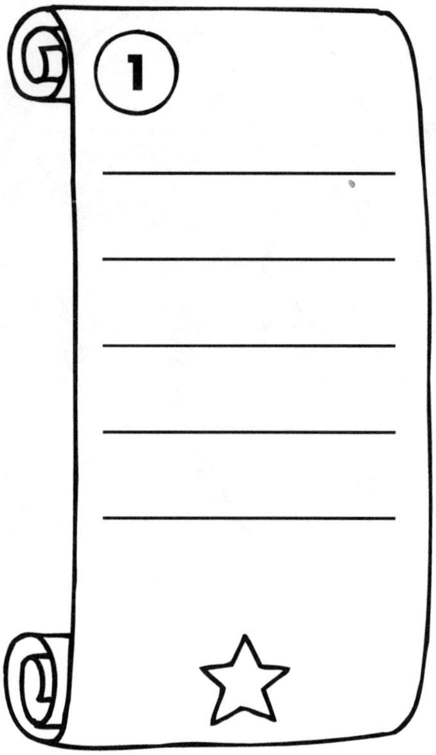

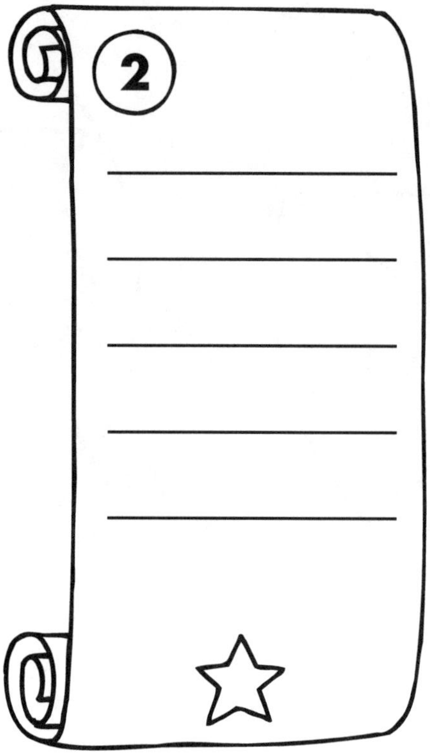

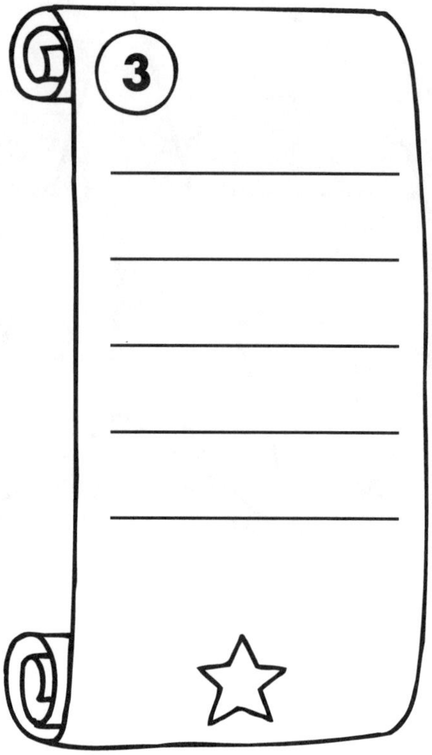

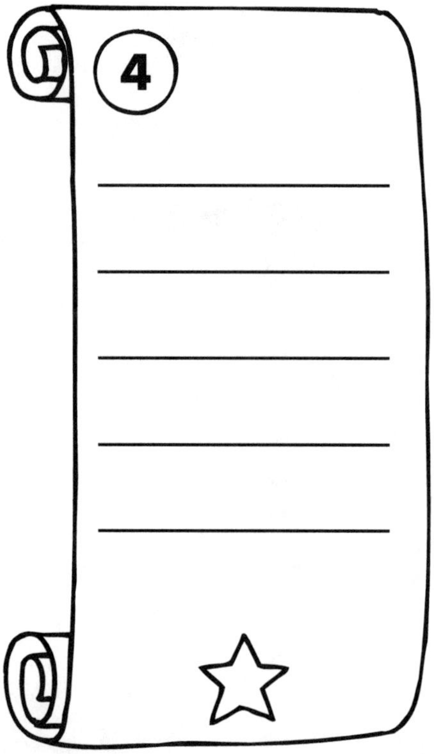

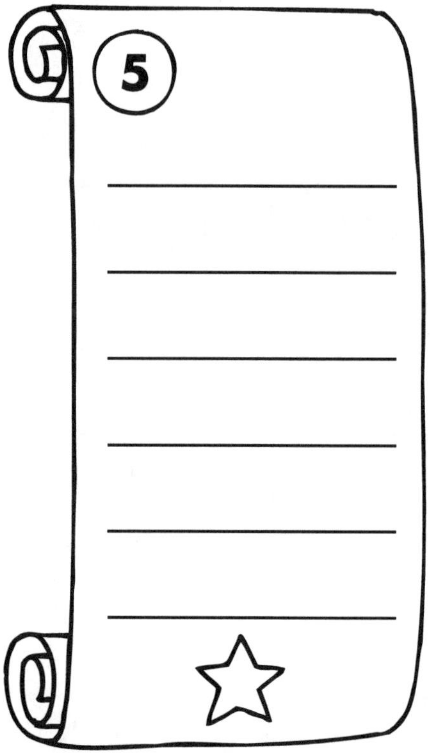

1	2	3	4	5
1	2	3	4	5
1	2	3	4	5
1	2	3	4	5
1	2	3	4	5
				6

ABC Snowmen

Alphabetical Order by Second Letter

Put the words in ABC order. Use the second letter. Pin the correct number to each word.

(Glue to oak tag and cut out.)

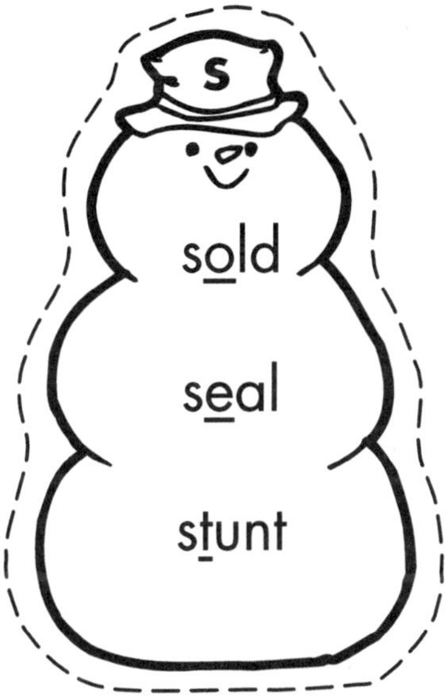

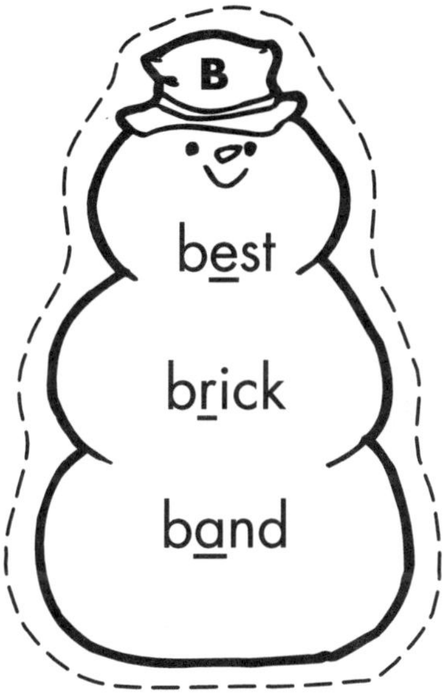

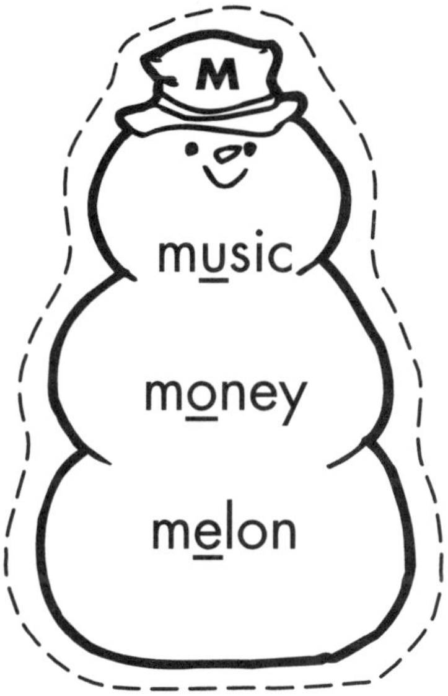

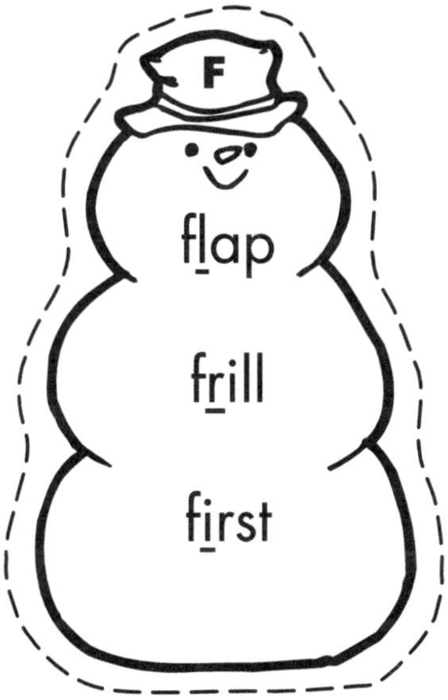

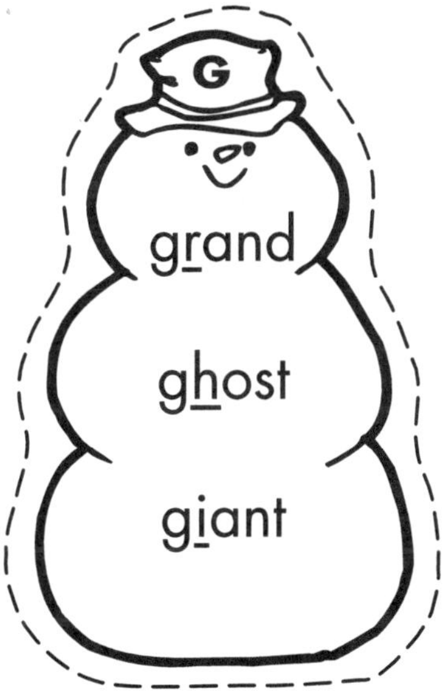

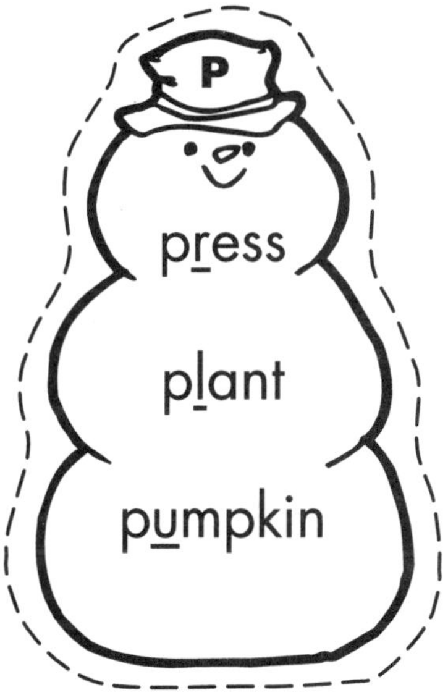

1	1	1	1	1	1
2	2	2	2	2	2
3	3	3	3	3	3

(Cut apart.
Glue to clothespin.)

ABC Wind-Up

Alphabet Order by Third Letter

ABC Wind-Up

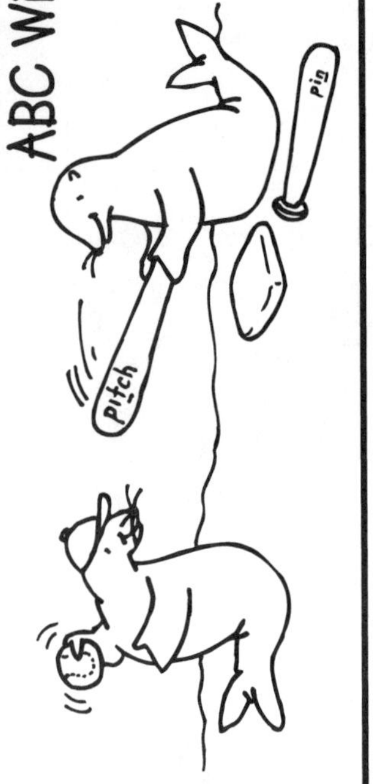

pepper
peaches
penalty
pewter
pelican

1
2
3
4
5

Use the third letter to put the words in ABC order. Draw a line from the number to the word.

ABC Wind-Up

latch
lawn
land
lace
lass

1
2
3
4
5

Use the third letter to put the words in ABC order. Draw a line from the number to the word.

ABC Ladders

Alphabetical Order by First and Second Letters

To Play:

Three can play. Shuffle the word cards and put them face down in the playing area. Each player takes an ABC Ladder and five cards, leaving cards face down until everyone has taken cards. When one of the players says "Go," all players turn their cards over. Players put their words in alphabetical order by first and second letters on the ABC Ladder starting at the top of the ladder. The first player to put his/her words in correct ABC order wins. There may be more than one winner. Players check each other for accuracy. They may play as many times as they wish, reshuffling the cards each time.

To Make:

Duplicate the game setup. Glue ABC Ladders and word cards to oak tag. Color and laminate if desired. Cut out the ladders and word cards. Store in a clasp manila envelope. Glue the playing directions to the front of the envelope.

ABC Ladders

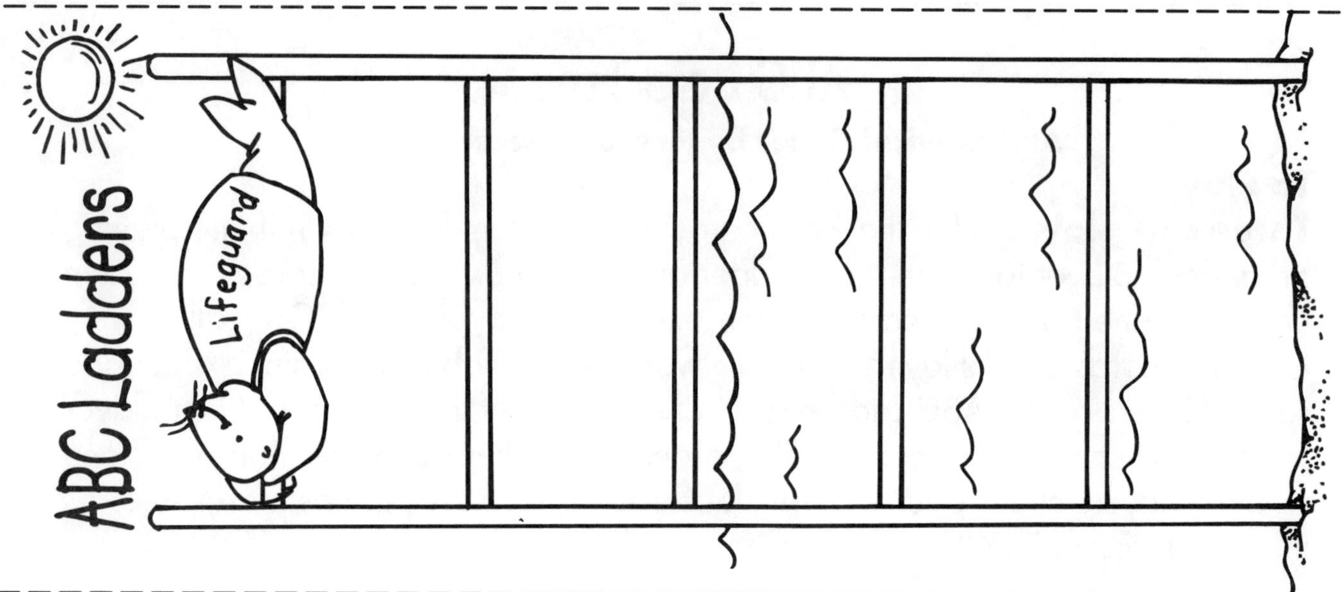

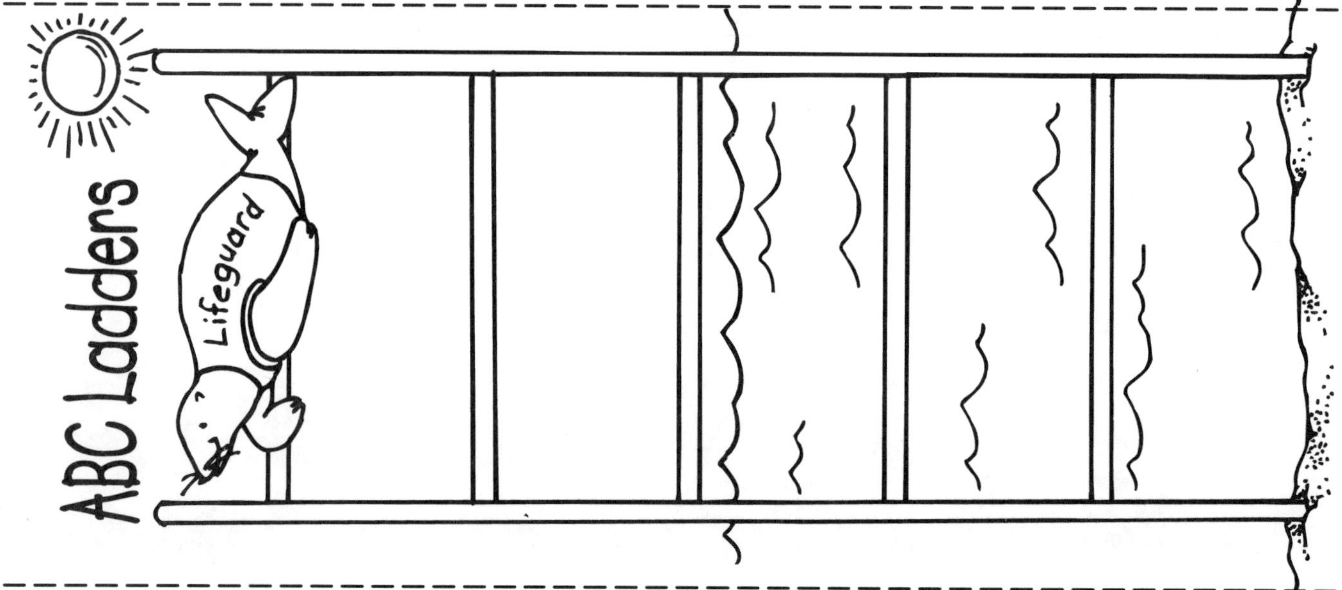

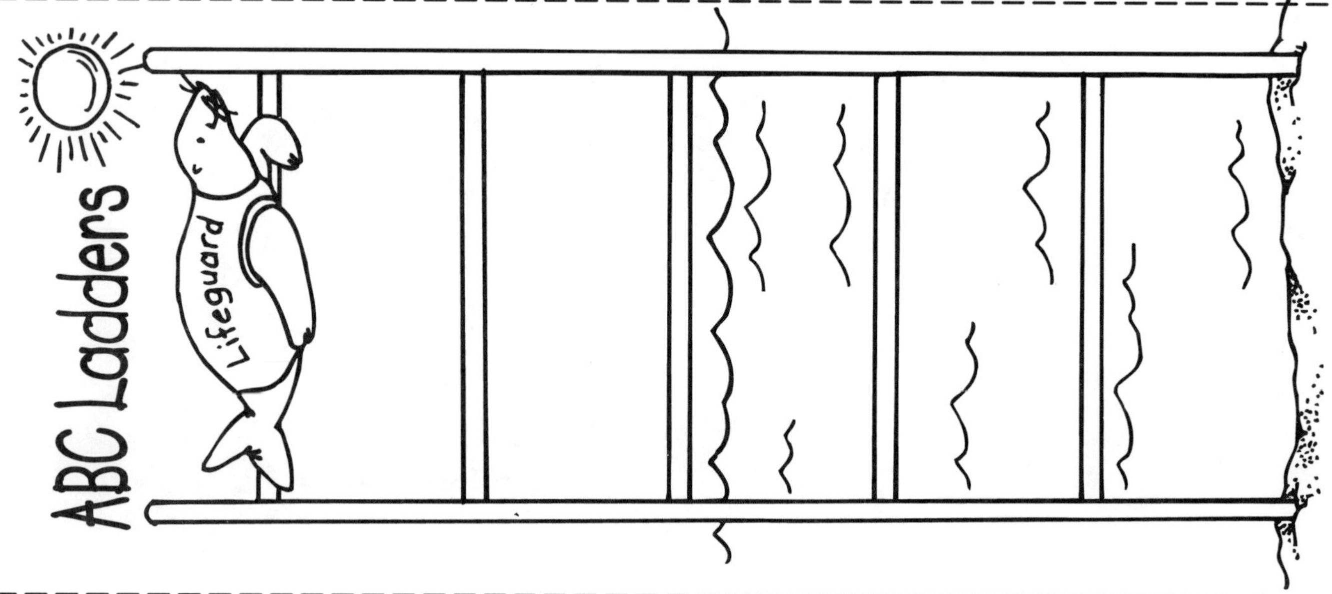

(Glue to oak tag. Cut on dotted lines.)

ABC Ladders

(Glue to oak tag. Cut on dotted lines.)

melon	November	October
pilot	rooster	sandbox
twenty	uncle	vase
Wednesday	yourself	zipper
dragon	nutmeg	clutter
twenty	umbrella	apple
breakfast	hoot	kettle
baker	library	moonlit
nutcracker	otter	phantom
remember	slowly	valley
wagon	zero	enter
joker	glare	tumble

ABC Ladders

(Glue to oak tag. Cut on dotted lines.)

ant	best	cliff
door	elf	frost
gift	help	ink
jump	kit	loft
mint	next	ox
plug	queen	ramp
stuck	tent	up
vent	west	x-ray
yellow	zest	always
bunny	cotton	finger
grandmother	Halloween	igloo
jingle	kangaroo	lemon

ABC Guide Words

65.

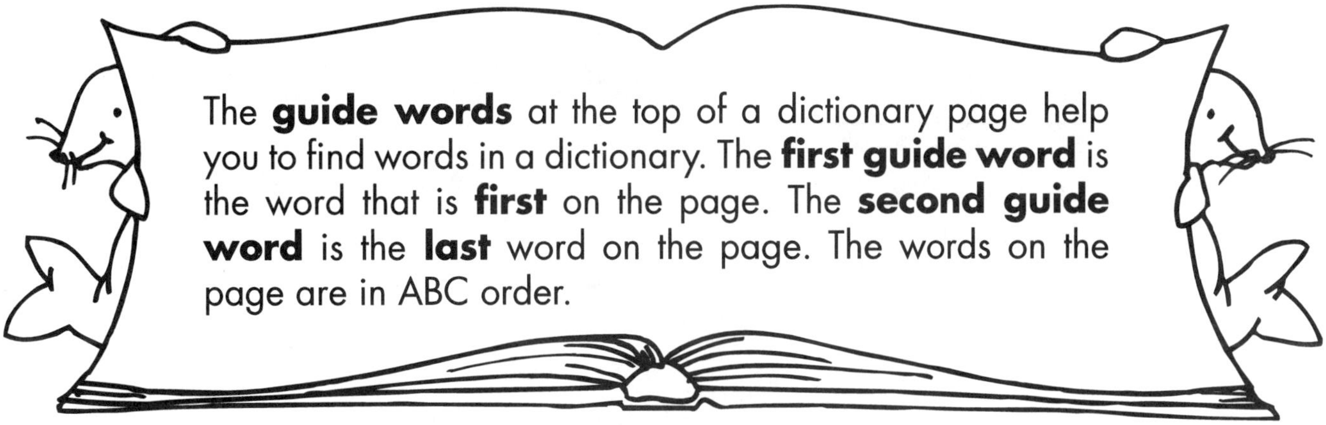

The **guide words** at the top of a dictionary page help you to find words in a dictionary. The **first guide word** is the word that is **first** on the page. The **second guide word** is the **last** word on the page. The words on the page are in ABC order.

Use the guide words to find the missing word that belongs on each page. Slip the word under the paper clip.

bacon _____ bait

- - - - -

ball _____ band

- - - - -

bash _____ bat

- - - - -

bluebell _____ boat

- - - - -

boiler _____ bone

- - - - -

brake _____ bread

- - - - -

(Glue sheet to oak tag. Cut slits on dotted lines. Clip a paper clip onto each slit. Cut words apart.)

bamboo	bold	basketball
brave	board	bag

The Sentence

A sentence is a group of words that tells a whole thought.

Read the groups of words below. Circle the ones that are sentences and tell a whole thought.

1. a dog
2. The sun was bright.
3. in the morning
4. I love picnics!
5. Can you play today?
6. my mom and dad
7. over the hill
8. Mark can ride a horse.

A part of the thought is missing in these sentences. Write in a word to make each sentence a whole thought.

1. Dennis and Phil ________________ to the ball game.
2. ________________ picked up the puppy.
3. Grandpa and Grandma ________________ on the farm.
4. Last night, I ____________________.
5. ________________ bought a brand new car.

The Subject and Action

A sentence must have a **subject** and an **action word.**
Sometimes the action word is in the form of "**be,**" as in **am**, **is**, **are**, and **was.**

Draw a line from the **subject** to the matching **action** part to make a complete thought or **sentence.** The first one is done.

1. The little boy	were packed.
2. A bunny	was haunted.
3. A tall green tree	like to rollerblade.
4. Two yellow birds	ran to his mother.
5. Tom and his friends	grew in the yard.
6. Our bags	sang in the tree.
7. The spooky house	hopped down the street.

Write one of the sentences you put together.

____

____

Capitals

Begin each sentence with a **capital letter.**

Summer is my favorite season.

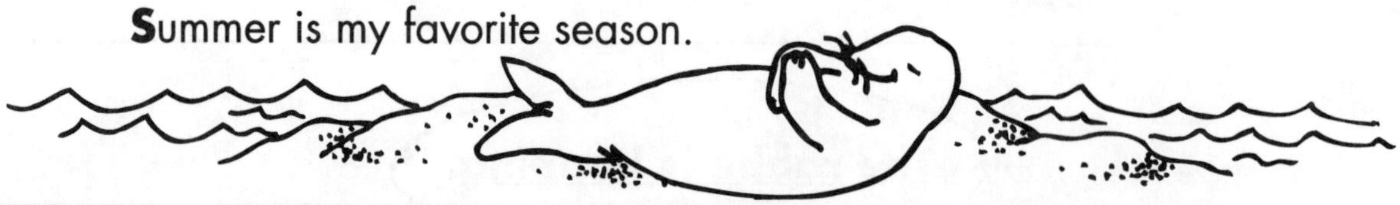

Begin all proper names of **people, places,** and **special names** with a **capital letter.** Read the examples under the labels.

People
Jim, **P**am, **M**ike
Dr. **S**mith
Mom and **D**ad

Places
New **Y**ork
Disneyland
Green **S**treet

Special Names
January
Monday
Valentine's **D**ay

Read the sentences. Draw three lines (≡) under letters that should be capitals. The number at the end of each sentence tells you how many capitals are needed.

1. mary, tom, and bob walk to school together. (3)

2. mr. martin left for paris on sunday. (4)

3. it was exciting to visit the empire state building. (4)

4. i am going to be a pirate on halloween. (2)

5. the trees are being trimmed on main street. (3)

6. my grandpa's birthday is in march. (3)

Write one of the sentences with the corrected capitals.

Punctuation

69.

End each sentence with a punctuation mark.

Put a **period** (.) at the end of a **telling sentence** or a **command**.

I read a good book today.
Please set the table.

Put a **question mark** (?) at the end of an **asking** sentence.

Is this your hat?

Put an **exclamation point** (!) at the end of a sentence that shows **excitement**.

We won the game!

Put a period (.), a question mark (?), or an exclamation point (!) at the end of each sentence. Circle the punctuation mark.

1. What will you buy at the toy store ? (circled)
2. That pie was delicious _____
3. May I have another piece _____
4. You may go out to play now _____
5. I can't wait for my next sleepover _____
6. It looks like it's going to rain today_____
7. We are all getting together for the holidays _____

The Paragraph

70.

A paragraph is a group of sentences about one main idea.

First: It begins with a **main idea sentence** that tells what the paragraph is going to be about.
Next: It has several **supporting sentences** that tell about the main idea.
Finally: It ends with a **concluding sentence** that reminds us what the main idea was about.

Main idea sentence: Muffy, my cat, is very frisky.
Supporting sentences: She jumps on my bed in the morning.
She likes batting a ball and chasing it.
She walks across the piano keys.
Concluding sentence: Muffy is active all day.

Indent the first line of a paragraph to show that a new idea is being introduced.

Indent One day, Muffy climbed to the top of a tree. She did not know how to get down. She mewed and mewed until Dad rescued her. Now Muffy is careful to scamper only halfway up a tree and come right down.

Read the next paragraph. Circle the **main idea** sentence.
Draw a line under all the **supporting** sentences.
Draw a box around the **concluding** sentence.

Digger, our pet alligator lizard, is fun to watch. It sleeps most of the day with one eye closed. Digger digs in the sand and climbs on the rocks in his tank. He eats live crickets that run around the tank. One day, he shed his skin backwards with the tail last! Digger doesn't seem to mind us looking at him all day.

The Main Idea

These supporting sentences need a main idea. Write the matching main idea sentence on the line.

Main Ideas

1. My grandmother spoils me.
2. School lunches are not for me.
3. I enjoy visits to the aquarium.
4. I like to ride on the train.

Main idea: ____

I love the dark, damp passageways.
I enjoy seeing the sea animals up close.
I am always surprised to see the different kinds of sea life.
It is like being in an undersea world.

Main idea: ____

The food is not tasty.
The sandwiches are soggy.
You can't always eat what you want.
Why do I have to eat school lunches?

Main idea: ____

I enjoy seeing the countryside whizzing by.
The clickety-clack of the train is soothing.
I can move around more freely.
It's great to be out of freeway traffic.

Main idea: ____

She makes my favorite things to eat.
She takes me shopping for new clothes.
She lets me sleep late in the morning.
Best of all, I never have to do chores.

Supporting Sentences

These main ideas need **supporting sentences**. Supporting sentences **tell about the main idea**. Write three supporting sentences for each main idea. The first supporting sentences are done for you.

The wind blew hard today.

It tossed trash cans around.

Large tree branches broke.

It was not safe to go out to play.

There are all kinds of bugs in this world.

A friend is someone who cares about you.

I wish I could be invisible.

The Concluding Sentence

73.

These paragraphs need a concluding sentence. Write the matching concluding sentence on the line below.

Concluding Sentences

1. Everyone should have music lessons.
2. I don't think I could live without it.
3. Gift wrapping makes me happy.
4. Finally, I climb into bed.

Getting ready for bed is a chore.
First, I have to brush my teeth.
Next, I have to get my pajamas on.
Then, I have to set out my clothes.

Concluding sentence: ______________________________

I love to wrap gifts.
I enjoy choosing the paper and ribbons.
I make great, curly bows.
I like to do a beautiful job.

Concluding sentence: ______________________________

The telephone is very useful.
It helps you to keep in touch with friends.
You can call for help in an emergency.
You can even check on the correct time.

Concluding sentence: ______________________________

Music lessons are good for everyone.
For one thing, they help you to listen carefully.
For another thing, you learn to follow directions.
Finally, you may find pleasure in playing or performing.

Concluding sentence: ______________________________

Something in the Sea

Sally Seal was sunning on the sand one day. All at once she saw something in the water! What was it?

Finish the drawing. Tell what Sally Seal saw. Write at least five sentences.

Deep Dark Cave

What is in this deep, dark cave? What is it doing there?

Finish the drawing. Tell what you think is in the cave. Write at least three to five sentences.

Mystery Boxes

What is inside these boxes? Why are they here?

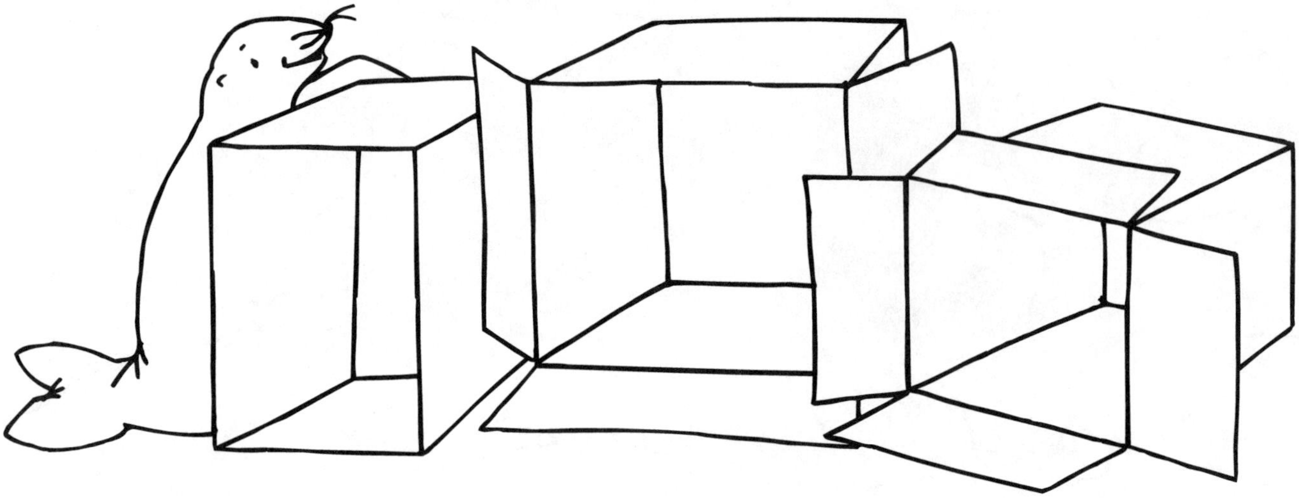

Draw what you think is in these boxes. Write about them and tell why they are here. Write at least five sentences.

Treasure Map

This treasure map belongs to you. What treasure will it help you find? How will you find it?

Finish the map. Put an X where the treasure is. Write how the map will help you find the treasure. Tell what the treasure is. Write five or more sentences.

Starting to Pre-Write

Brainstorming

Before you begin to write, **BRAINSTORM!** Think of everything you can on the subject you plan to write about. **List** all the things you think of. See the samples below

Night	Rain	Dogs
dark	pitter-patter	bark
late	drops	small, big
quiet	cold, wet	walks
sleepy	puddles	bite
bed	mud	tails
cozy	raincoats	friend
moon	umbrella	play

Now it's your turn to **brainstorm.** Write as many things as you can think of for the subjects below.

Camping	Homework	Clouds
______	______	______
______	______	______
______	______	______
______	______	______
______	______	______

If you need more space, turn the paper over.

Brainstorming on Your Own

Choose two topics from the box or choose two of your own. Brainstorm and list your ideas on each topic.

Cats	Dreams	Sports	Books
Friends	Cartoons	Rollerblading	Rock Music

Topic ____

Brainstorm

____________	____________	____________	____________
____________	____________	____________	____________
____________	____________	____________	____________
____________	____________	____________	____________
____________	____________	____________	____________
____________	____________	____________	____________
____________	____________	____________	____________

Topic ____

Brainstorm

____________	____________	____________	____________
____________	____________	____________	____________
____________	____________	____________	____________
____________	____________	____________	____________
____________	____________	____________	____________
____________	____________	____________	____________
____________	____________	____________	____________
____________	____________	____________	____________

Starting to Pre-Write

Webbing

Webbing is another useful way to **BRAINSTORM** before you write.

You can use a **web** to **brainstorm.** The name of your subject or topic goes in the big circle on the **web.** The ideas about the topic go in the little circles around the web. Finish this web on the topic of **Halloween** by writing in your ideas.

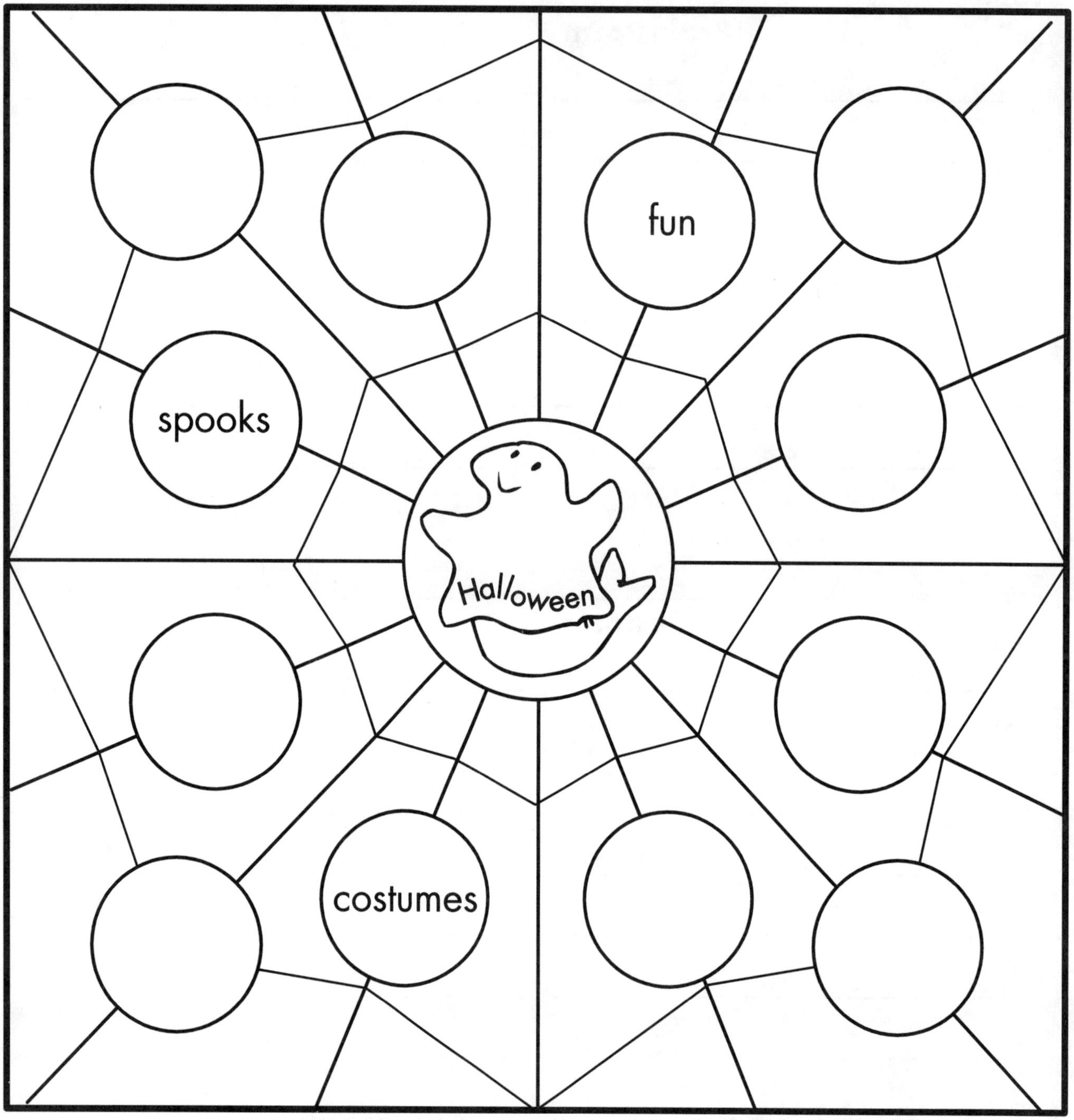

Webbing Form

81.

Choose a topic of your own and **brainstorm** using the **web.** Write your subject or topic in the big circle on the **web.** Write your **ideas** about the topic in the little circles on the **web.** Add more circles if you need to.

Starting to Organize

Grouping

After you **brainstorm** and list everything you can think of on a subject, you need to **group** your ideas and give each group a name or label.

Our subject or topic is **Favorite Foods.** Here is a list of ideas.

Favorite Foods

cake	ice cream	fish
spaghetti	steak	chow mein
hamburgers	apple pie	ravioli
macaroni	fried chicken	chocolate pudding

The ideas fall into three groups: **Pasta, Meats,** and **Desserts.** Write the label for each group and list the ideas under the label. The first group is done for you. Finish the other two groups.

Favorite Foods

Pasta	____________	____________
spaghetti	____________	____________
macaroni	____________	____________
chow mein	____________	____________
ravioli	____________	____________

Starting to Organize 83.

Ordering

When you begin to write, you need to know the **order** of the ideas you are going to write about. You can show the **order** by numbering each group of ideas **1, 2, 3,** and so on.

It is a sunny day and a perfect day to wash the dog. Which idea would you write about first? Order the ideas by putting **1, 2, or 3** in the ( ).

Washing the Dog

Washing ( )	Getting Materials ( )	Drying ( )
soap the dog	big tub	dog out of tub
scrub	soap	towel dry
rinse	warm water	brush hair
empty tub	brush	play in the sun

We all have our favorite days of the week. What are your three (3) **favorite days** choosing from Sunday, Monday, Tuesday, Wednesday, Thursday, Friday, and Saturday? Why? Write the **days** and the **order** in which you would write about them—1, 2, or 3. **Brainstorm** ideas and write them under the days.

Favorite Days

______ ( )	______ ( )	______ ( )
Day	Day	Day
______	______	______
______	______	______
______	______	______
______	______	______

Starting to Write

Write-Ups

84.

After you have **brainstormed, grouped, and ordered** your ideas, you can start to write up your ideas.

We will use the **Favorite Foods groups** of ideas with their labels from the Starting to Write: Grouping activity. These are our **notes.** They have been numbered in the **order** in which they are to be written about .

Favorite Foods

Pasta (1)	Meats (2)	Desserts (3)
spaghetti	steak	cake
macaroni	hamburgers	chocolate pudding
chow mein	fish	pie
ravioli	fried chicken	ice cream

Favorite Foods

I have three favorite foods. The first food that I enjoy is pasta, especially spaghetti, macaroni, chow mein, and meaty ravioli. The second food I like is meat, which includes steak, hamburgers, fish, and crispy fried chicken. Last but best of all are the dessert foods. My favorites are vanilla ice cream, chocolate pudding, and hot apple pie. Just thinking about my favorite foods makes me very hungry!

On the next page is another grouping of brainstormed ideas. **Write up** the ideas in the order in which they are numbered on the Write-Up Form.

Write-Ups

Here is a group of ideas on the topic **Summer.** Use them as notes. Write up the ideas in the order in which they are numbered. You may add to the lists or add any words that will make your write-up more interesting or clear. Use the **Write-Up Form**.

Summer

Relax (1)	Activities (2)	Trips (3)
sleep late	sports	beach
friends over	computer	to grandparents
stay up late	shopping	amusement park

Write-Up Form

Summer

Topic

Summer is my favorite season for several reasons. First, I can relax in the summer. I can ______________________________

____

____

Second, I can ______________________________

____

____

____

Finally, ______________________________

____

____

______________________________.

If you need more space, use the back of this page.

Brainstorm, Group, Order! **86.**

Choose a topic of your own. Brainstorm, group your ideas, and show the order you will be using to write about them.

Topic ______________________

Brainstorm

Group and Order

( ) ( ) ( )

The Manatee

The manatee is a giant sea mammal. It has a grayish-brown body that is 10 feet long. A full-grown manatee weighs between 1,000 and 3,000 pounds. The manatee looks like a potato with flippers and a paddletail. The manatee has a snouty nose with wide nostrils and stiff bristle hairs around it.

The manatee lives in warm waters three to ten feet deep. It can live in both fresh and salt water on the coast or in rivers. In the winter, the manatee moves to warm waters where there is plenty of sea grass.

The manatee is often called a sea cow because it grazes on sea grass at the bottom of shallow water. In six to eight hours, a manatee can eat 100 pounds of sea grass. Between feedings, the manatee sleeps floating on the top of the water or at the bottom of a river or stream.

The manatee is a very loving creature and often can be seen giving kisses to its young and playing with them. It is a peaceful, friendly animal and will not fight even to protect its young. It is also a curious animal and often likes to check things out.

The manatee is an endangered animal. There are only 1,200 manatees left in Florida waters. The danger comes mostly from man. Man pollutes the waters the manatees swim in. Manatees often get tangled in trap and fishing lines while nosing around them or get trapped in floodgates.

Although manatees are strong swimmers, they are slow moving. They are not able to get out of the way of speeding motorboats fast enough. Many manatees have been injured or killed by the propellers of these boats.

Sea World rescue teams in Florida have saved and cared for many manatees, and the fight to save them goes on. Laws have been passed to protect the manatee and to make the water a safer place for manatees to live.

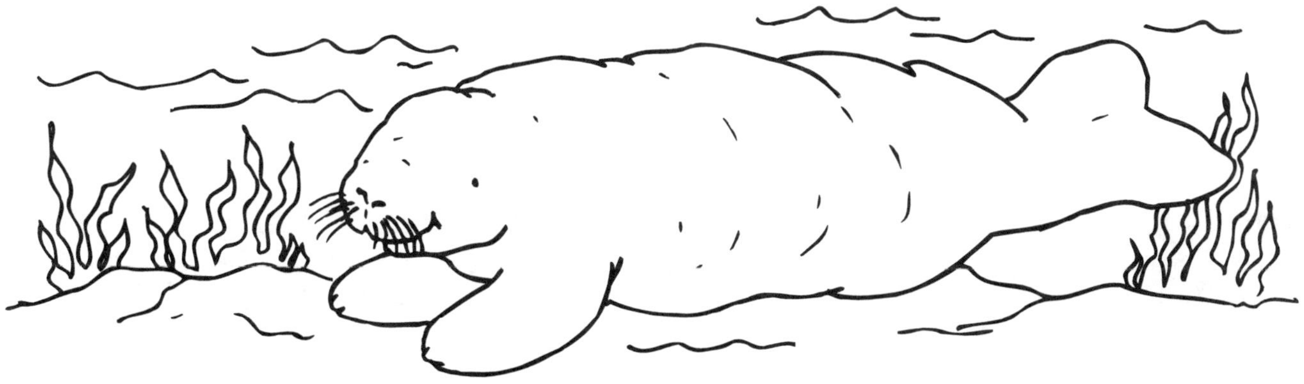

Taking Notes for The Manatee **88.**

Read the story **The Manatee.** Complete the notes under the labels below. The notes go with the **main idea sentence** below. Some of the note-taking has been done for you. Fill in the report write-up on the next page.

____

(Subject)

The manatee is an unusual sea mammal.

(Main idea sentence)

Its size (1)	**The way it looks** (2)	**The way it acts** (3)
• is	•	• is
• is		• is
• weighs	• has	• is
	• with	• is
		• will

Use your information to fill in this report.

The Manatee

The manatee is an unusual sea mammal. First, the manatee is a ____________________ mammal. It is ______________ long. It weighs ___________________. Second, it has a strange shape and looks ____________ ____ ____. Third, it acts in special ways. It is _________________, ____________________, ____________________, and is a very _________________________ animal. It will not even _______________________. There are only a small number of this odd-looking but gentle sea mammal left in the world.

You may want to **rewrite** this report with **your own main idea and notes.** Use the **note-taking** and the **write-up** pages.

The Elephant Seal

If you ever visit Ano Nuevo Point in California you can see an amazing sea mammal, the elephant seal. It is called the elephant seal because it is very large and has a lumpy, long nose or **proboscis** (pro-bah-sis). Its **proboscis** can be one to two feet long. Its huge, round body has four flippers. The adult male can weigh up to 6,000 pounds. In water, the elephant seal moves gracefully and can make deep dives down to 2,100 feet below sea level. It is clumsier on land. It bumps along the sand using its front fins.

Elephants seals generally live alone. They swim and feed on fish and squid along the coast. However, from December to March the males and females come together on land to mate. Adult males or **bulls** arrive first. They use their proboscis to make loud snorting noises to challenge each other.

The females or **cows** arrive next. They group themselves into **harems** of about 25 to 50 females. Each female gives birth to a seal **pup.** The mother sings to it when it is born. The pup yaps back. In this way, mother and pup can find each other by their sounds.

A **bull** must fight to mate with his harem. He makes a loud roar, using his **proboscis** to make it noiser and scarier. If another bull answers, they fight. Chest to chest, they use their body to hit each other with strong blows. They bite each other with their sharp teeth. The battle is over when one seal backs off. The winner mates with all the females in his harem. He becomes a **beachmaster** or an **alpha bull.** He is usually the biggest and strongest bull with the largest **proboscis** and the loudest roar.

Soon after the pups are born, the seals return to the sea, leaving the pups behind. In a few months the pups head for the sea. For several months the seals spend all their time at sea but come back on land to molt and mate again.

Taking Notes for The Elephant Seal 91.

Read the story **The Elephant Seal**. Finish writing the notes under the labels. The notes go with the **main idea** sentence below. Some of the note-taking has been done for you. Then fill in the report write-up.

____
(Subject)

The male elephant seal is an amazing mammal.
(Main idea sentence)

Body size (1)	**Its nose** (2)	**Its mating habits** (3)
• is	• body	
• weighs	• nose	•
	• long	• makes
		using its nose
		• with body
		• with teeth
		• winner

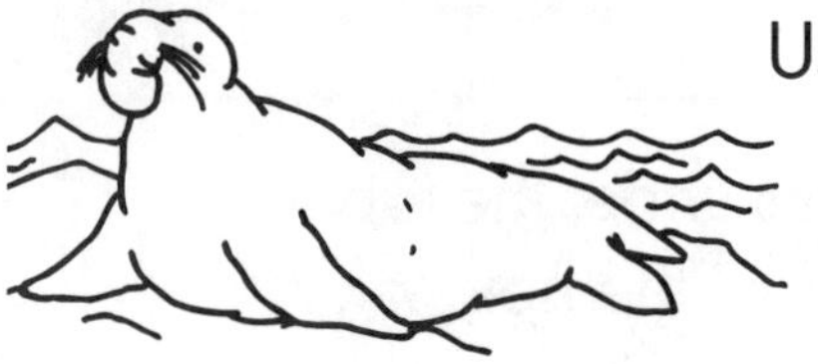

Use your information to fill in this report.

The Elephant Seal

The male elephant seal is an amazing mammal.

One amazing thing is its size. The male elephant seal is very ____________. It can weigh up to ____________ pounds. It has a ______________, ______________ body. Another amazing thing is its ____________ or ____________. It is ____________, ____________, and ____________. It can be ____________ long. The last amazing thing is that the elephant seal must __________ in order to mate. First, it tries to scare off other males by making a loud ______________ using its nose. Next, it ______________ using its big ______________. It ______________ with its sharp ____________. The winner can ___________ with all the females in his harem. You can watch this fascinating sea mammal at Ano Nuevo Point in California.

You may want to **rewrite** this report with **your own main idea and notes.** Use the **note-taking** and the **write-up** pages.

The Sea Otter

Sea otters, the smallest of sea mammals, were once hunted and killed to extinction. Today, protected by laws, the four-feet long sleek, brown, furry bodies once again dive, swim, and play along the coasts of Japan, Siberia, and the Pacific. Their round flat faces, small ears, beady eyes, and long whiskers can once more be seen peeking out of the sea water.

With its four paws and slim body, the sea otter swims and dives fast. It uses its webbed hind legs like oars or paddles. It can stay under water for about five minutes. Since its body uses up food fast, it must hunt and eat often. It turns over rocks and stones at the bottom of the sea with its front paws, looking for abalones, crabs, sea urchins, and shellfish. It brings the food up to the surface of the water and eats it while floating on its back. Using its chest as a table, it cracks open shellfish with stones. It tears out bits of meat with its front paws and teeth to eat.

Sea otters spend all their time in the water, hunting, playing, mating, giving birth, and resting. To rest, they float on their backs with seaweed wrapped around their bodies to keep them from floating away. Their thick coat of fur traps air to keep them warm and dry. To mate, the female otter finds a mate from among the large groups of otters living at sea. One baby is born eight or nine months later on a bed of floating seaweed.

The mother otter keeps the baby on her tummy where it nurses on her milk. When she wants to dive for food, she wraps the cub with strands of seaweed and ties it to a floating cradle of kelp. Or she may dive with the cub tucked under her arm. When escaping from an enemy, she holds the cub in her mouth by its neck and swims away to safety. When the cub is six months old, the mother feeds it bits of meat from crabs and clams. She teaches the cub how to hunt and dive. Within a year, the young sea otter can find its own food and face the world by itself.

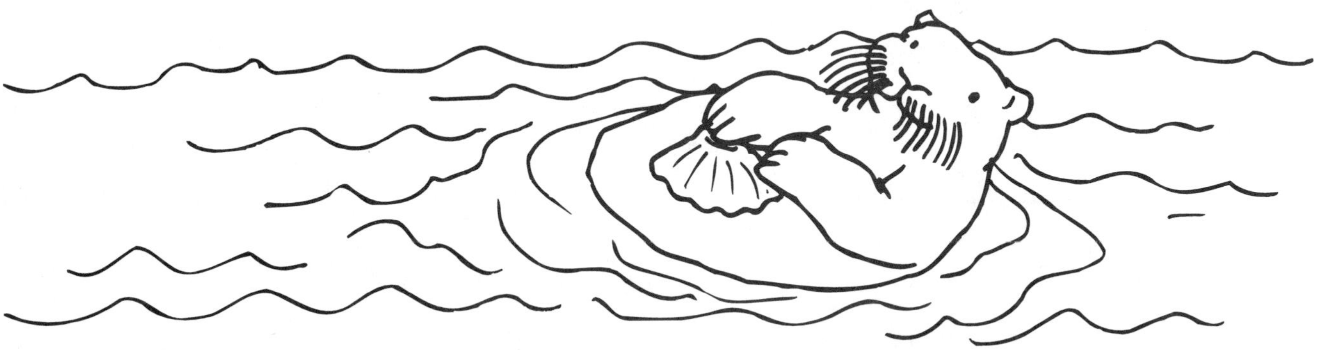

Taking Notes for The Sea Otter

Read the story **The Sea Otter**. Complete the notes under the labels below. The notes go with the **main idea sentence** below. Some of the note-taking has been done for you. Then fill in the report write-up.

____
(Subject)

The sea otter has interesting habits.
(Main idea sentence)

Hunts (1)

- **dives**
- turns

Eats (2)

- looks
- uses
- cracks

Rests (3)

- tears
-
- wraps

Raises cubs (4)

- baby on
- baby
- teaches

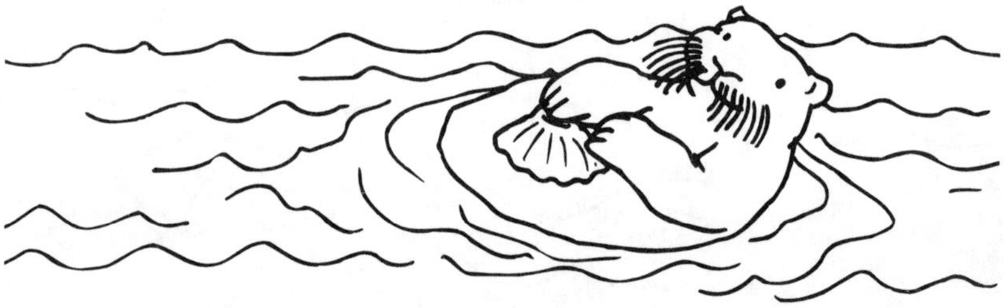

Use your information to fill in this report.

The Sea Otter

The sea otter has interesting habits. To hunt, the

sea otter__________________________________. It

looks for_____________________________________

____.

To eat, it ____________________. It cracks __________

____.

It tears ______________________________________.

To rest, it ____________________________________.

It wraps______________________________________.

To raise her cubs, the mother otter___________________

____.

She teaches the cub______________________________.

The way the sea otter lives is fascinating.

You may want to **rewrite** this report with **your own main idea and notes.** Use the **note-taking and the write-up** pages.

Choose a topic of your own. **Read** about it. Decide what facts you want to report on. Then **take notes. Write up** your report.

96.

Taking Notes for a Report

Write **labels** for the things you want to find out. Write your notes under the labels. Show in the (   ) in what **order** you will write up each group of facts.

Subject

(   ) (   ) (   )

Use another note-taking page for more groups of facts.

Name ______________________ Date ______________________ **97.**

Write-Up Form

____

Topic

If you need more space, use the back of this page.

Answer Key

Note-taking for a Short Report on The Manatee

88.

Read the story "The Manatee." Complete the notes under the labels below. The notes go with the **main idea sentence** below. Some of the note-taking has been done for you. Fill in the report write-up on the next page.

Manatee
(Subject)

The manatee is an unusual sea mammal.
(Main idea sentence)

Its size (1)	**The way it looks** (2)	**The way it acts** (3)
• is **a giant mammal**	• **like a potato with flip-**	• is **loving**
• is **ten feet long**	**pers and a paddletail**	• is **friendly**
• weighs **1,000-**	• has **a snouty nose**	• is **curious**
3000 pounds	• with **stiff hairs**	• is **peaceful**
		• will **not fight**

Use your information to fill in this report.

89.

The Manatee

The manatee is an unusual sea mammal. First, the manatee is a **giant** mammal. It is **ten feet** long. It weighs **1,000 to 3,000 pounds**. Second, it has a strange shape and looks **like a potato with flippers and a paddle tail.** Third, it acts in special ways. It is **loving**, **friendly**, **peaceful**, and is a very **curious** animal. It will not even **fight**. There are only a small number of this odd-looking but gentle sea mammal left in the world.

You may want to **rewrite** this report with **your own main idea and notes.** Use the **note-taking** and the **write-up** pages

Note-taking for a Short Report on The Elephant Seal 91.

Read the story on **The elephant seal.** Finish writing the notes under the labels. The notes go with the **main idea** sentence below. Some of the note-taking has been done for you. Fill in the report write-up on the next page.

The Elephant Seal
(Subject)

The male elephant seal is an amazing mammal.
(Main idea sentence)

Body size (1)	**Its nose** (2)	**Its mating habits** (3)
• is **large**	• **lumpy, long** nose	• **fights**
• weighs **6000 pounds**	• **one to two feet** long	• makes **a loud**
• **huge, round** body		**roar** using its nose
		• **hits** with body
		• **bites** with teeth
		• winner **mates with**
		females

Use your information to fill in this report. **92.**

The Elephant Seal

The male elephant seal is an amazing mammal.

One amazing thing is its size. The male elephant seal is very **large**. It can weigh up to **6000** pounds. It has a **huge**, **round** body. Another amazing thing is its **nose** or **proboscis**. It is **lumpy**, and **long**. It can be **one to two feet** long. The last amazing thing is that the elephant seal must **fight** in order to mate. First, it tries to scare off other males by making a loud **roar** using its nose. Next, it **hits** using its big **body**. It **bites** with its sharp **teeth**. The winner can **mate** with all the females in his harem. You can watch this fascinating sea mammal at Ano Nuevo Point in California.

You may want to **rewrite** this report with **your own main idea and notes.** Use the **note-taking** and the **write-up** pages

Note-taking for a Short Report on The Sea Otter **94.**

Read the story on the sea otter. Complete the notes under the labels below. The notes go with the **main idea sentence** below. Some of the note-taking has been done for you. Fill in the report write-up on the next page

The Sea Otter
(Subject)

The sea otter has interesting habits.
(Main idea sentence)

Hunts (1)	**Eats** (2)	**Rests** (3)
• **dives**	• uses **chest as table**	• **floats on its back**
• turns **over rocks, stones**	• cracks **shellfish with stones**	• wraps **seaweed around itself**
• looks **for abalones, crabs, and shellfish**	• tears **bits of meat with paws**	

Raises cubs (4)
- baby on **mother's tummy**
- **nurses** baby
- teaches **cub how to hunt and dive**

Use your information to fill in this report. **95.**

The Sea Otter

The sea otter has interesting habits. To hunt, the sea otter **dives and turns over rocks and stones**. It looks for **albalones, crabs, and shellfish**.

To eat, it **uses its chest as a table**.

It cracks **shellfish with stones**.

It tears **bits of meat with its claws and teeth**.

To rest, it **floats on its back**.

It wraps **seaweed around its body so it will not float away**.

To raise her cubs, the mother otter **puts the baby on her tummy and nurses it**.

She teaches the cub **how to hunt and dive**.

The way the sea otter lives is fascinating.

You may want to **rewrite** this report with **your own main idea and notes.** Use the **note-taking and the write-up** pages.